Reiki Rays

REIKI 101

101 Answers for Your Reiki Questions

Angie Webster, Patti Deschaine
Haripriya Suraj, Deborah Lloyd,
Ashwita Goel

Copyright

© 2016, Acorn Gecko SRL

ALL RIGHTS RESERVED. This book contains material protected under International and Federal Copyright Laws and Treaties. Any unauthorized reprint or use of this material is prohibited. No part of this book may be reproduced or transmitted in any form or by any means, electronic or mechanical, including photocopying, recording, or by any information storage and retrieval system without express written permission from the publisher.

Reiki is not a replacement for medical assistance. Always seek professional medical support if you experience anything that requires it. Seek the services of a competent professional if expert assistance is required.

To fully understand and to be able to apply the techniques described in this book, the reader should already be introduced to the healing magic of Reiki.

Table of Contents

Before You Begin 7
Chapter 1 – The Most Important Question of All 8
   How is Reiki different and why would Reiki work where other things have failed? 9
Chapter 2 – Explaining Reiki 14
   How to explain Reiki to others? 15
   How to explain distance healing to others? 17
   How to explain Reiki to teenage children? 18
Chapter 3 – Hand Positions 19
   Why do we need hand positions? 21
   Is it necessary to go through all the hand positions when giving a Reiki treatment? 22
   How long should we send healing in each hand position and why? 23
Chapter 4 – Does Reiki Work 24
   How do I know if Reiki is working? 25
   How can you tell, or know, that you are actually doing Reiki? 27
   How do you go about getting back into practicing Reiki after a break? How do you make it stronger and more effective? 29
   Does Reiki flow while having hands or legs crossed? 30
   Can Reiki still flow when performing a healing session if the practitioner has carpal tunnel? 31
Chapter 5 – Self Healing 32
   If you don't have much time to do Reiki, what are most important things that should be done? 33
   Should you go through the entire process of calling the Reiki energy every time you are doing self-treatment? 34
   If I do Reiki only once in a while, is it as effective (each time) as when it's done frequently? 35
   Why am I falling asleep during self-healing sessions? 36
   I practice self-healing daily. Why do I still get sick? 38
   What to do when you get sick as a Reiki Master? 40
   What is the best way to heal yourself using Reiki if you have anxiety / panic attacks? 41
Chapter 6 – Symbols 42
   If Reiki is universal healing energy, why do we need special symbols or an attunement process to open ourselves up to this flow? 43
   Are the symbols manipulating the Reiki energy? 45

Is it necessary to draw the symbols on your palms and on your client? 46
Can you use some symbols without initiation? 47

Chapter 7 – Distance Healing 48
How to proceed when someone on Facebook asks for a healing? 49
How does Reiki find its way to someone who gives just an initial? 50
Are the intuitions I get during distance Reiki healing sessions true? 51
Is there some way to "compress" time and do what would be a 60 minutes healing session in less time? 52
Does healing work when receiving Reiki on YouTube? 53

Chapter 8 – Attunements 54
Does one get any indication of the flow of energy after an attunement? 55
How can I know for sure if the remote attunement was really performed? 56
What is the right way to attune a student and what role does intuition play in the attunement process? 57
Should Reiki be completed in the one lineage? 59
What is the earliest age that a person can be attuned to Reiki? 60
How do I start attuning others and what are the ways to give attunements to students? 61
Is it possible to be attuned by video? Does it work? 62
What are the advantages / disadvantages of being attuned in one Reiki type over another? 63
Why can't I use Karuna® Reiki if I'm attuned to Usui Reiki? 65

Chapter 9 – Reiki Practice 67
How do I know when I am ready and able to provide Reiki healing sessions on others? 68
How do I get over my insecurity regarding offering Reiki? 69
Do I always need to be in a certain frame of mind to perform Reiki? 70
What should I be thinking or saying inside my head while I give a Reiki session? 71
How do you keep your mind focused on treating your client during your Reiki sessions? 73
Do you work on the body 'system' where the dis-ease started, or do you just treat as a whole? 74
Why does the client's pain increase after a Reiki session and what to do about it? 75
Why does Reiki feel warm some times, and cold other times? 77
Why am I getting pain in a certain area while doing Reiki for a client? 79

What are the meanings of sensations I feel when giving a Reiki treatment? 80
What can I do to increase my sensitivity to Reiki? 82
What can I do to be able to do Byosen Scan? 85
How can one learn to scan aura? 87
Should the healer continue giving Reiki or stop when the client experiences a healing crisis? 89
Is it possible to give Reiki to a group of people all at once? How would one go about that? 90
How to approach Reiki on someone who says they are ready to receive Reiki but energetically they are not? 92
Is it all right to send Reiki to someone without their permission? 93
Is it better for the client to be lying down or seated? 94
I used to practice until I was diagnosed with fibromyalgia and lupus. Am I right to feel that I must clear myself so that I can begin practicing again? 95

Chapter 10 – Protection 96
How do you know if you're using your own energy during healing? 97
Can the practitioner absorb negative energy from the client? 98
Do healers get the clients' disease, or are interfering with that person's karma? 100
How do I protect myself from picking up client's energy? 101
What is the best shielding and best grounding mechanism when giving a client Reiki? 104
Is it possible to repel an energy vampire using Reiki? 105

Chapter 11 – Business and Marketing 106
How do you find the first paying clients? 107
How does one differentiate themselves from other practitioners? 109
How do I get my Reiki clients to come back for regular treatment? ... 111
What is the best way to ensure your safety? 112

Chapter 12 – Reiki as Complementary Therapy 114
Is Reiki effective against chronic conditions (Cancer, MS, Diabetes, etc.)? 115
Is it advisable to do Reiki on someone with cancer? 116
How to give Reiki for Parkinson's disease patients? 117
How does Reiki help in treating autism? 119
Can Reiki help when dealing with severe depression? 121
Do antidepressants hinder the Reiki connection? 122
Does Reiki help with menopause? 123
Does Reiki help with arthritis? 124

Chapter 13 – Relationships 125
   How do you use Reiki to manifest a life partner? 126
   Does Reiki work for broken relationships? 127
   How to use cord cutting and Reiki to disconnect from a relationship? 128

Chapter 14 – Job / Career 130
   How can Reiki help when looking for a new job? 131
   How can Reiki help me to find and settle with a good job, or a promotion at my current job? 134

Chapter 15 – Healing the Past 135
   How do I heal past harm I have caused? 136
   How to heal a past life trauma? 138

Chapter 16 – Death 139
   Can Reiki assist a client to pass over more easily? 140
   Is there any special way to administer healing during final days of someone? 141
   Can Reiki be given to the departed souls? 142
   Why is that I have a fear of death? 143

Chapter 17 – Angels 145
   How can I connect with my guardian angel? 146

Chapter 18 – Spirituality 147
   What is the difference between Reiki and Spiritual Healing? 148
   What is the difference between Reiki and the Divine / God? 149
   Does Reiki have any connection with Jesus? 150

Chapter 19 – Miscellaneous 151
   My Reiki training only took 4 hours. Is my Reiki as good as others' who have done 2 days? 152
   What is Breath Reiki? 153
   What does it mean to infuse something with Reiki? 154
   Why is it advised to receive Reiki from others, like a Reiki circle, even though self-treatments are performed regularly? 155
   How long will the Reiki energy stay in an object? 156
   Why are my dreams so vivid since I have resumed self-treatment? 157
   Can Reiki be used to harm people? 158
   Is there such a thing as 'overloading' yourself with Reiki energy? 159
   How do I heal effects I feel during Full Moon? 160
   Is this possible to learn or practice Reiki during pregnancy? 161
   What's with the negative messages on Reiki on the Internet? ... 162

Chapter 20 – Life Purpose 163
   Is there a way to use Reiki to help determine your Life Purpose? 164

About the Authors 166

Before You Begin

Before you start reading this book... THANK YOU!

Thank you for your interest in Reiki, thank you for making the world a better place, thank you for purchasing this book.

We asked our readers what were their questions about Reiki, and compiled a list of the most popular questions. Our dear Reiki featured authors Angie Webster, Patti Deschaine, Haripriya Suraj, Deborah Lloyd, and Ashwita Goel kindly and joyfully answered the questions.

The first question has five answers, one from each author. Subsequent questions have one answer, or in some cases two.

We hope this book will help you deepen your understanding of Reiki, and move further on your spiritual path.

We also take this opportunity to extend our heartfelt thanks to all our Reiki authors, who amongst themselves have spent thousands of hours sharing their wisdom and experience with the Reiki community.

Blessings!
Maria and Gec Diaconu - Reiki Rays

Chapter 1 – The Most Important Question of All

Question 1

How is Reiki different and why would Reiki work where other things have failed?

I have tried lots of things, I have used the scientific approach, I have tried spiritual things, and I have tried things that combined the two. Many of them seemed to work, at least for a while, but eventually I felt that something was off, or for some reason or another it stopped working. **How is Reiki different and why would Reiki work where other things have failed?**

Angie's answer:

The honest answer is that it's possible that Reiki may not work in the way that you expect it to. Reiki accesses the Life Force that supports all of life, so it seems very spiritual in that sense. It's beyond our current scientific comprehension. We get closer with the study of quantum physics, but we still don't understand and it's possible we never will.

Yet, what Reiki does for us on a physical level is very practical. During Reiki, the body very quickly settles into a deeply relaxed state, letting go of the typical stressful state we all live in. This alone activates the body's natural systems for healing. We all have the inborn state of 'rest and restore mode' in which we naturally repair and regenerate. It is the opposite of 'fight or flight'. In this state, the mind eases and sees more clearly. Reiki has been shown to reduce anxiety and pain enough that it is often used during cancer treatment and after surgery in many hospitals to increase the comfort of patients. This often reduces the need for pain medication and decreases recovery time.

With the method of Reiki, Life Force energy works with your own energy to bring about the best possible healing outcome for you. That is a very individual thing, so it means something different for everyone. It may not mean the difficulty is "cured" or goes away. Rather than seeking a specific outcome or cure, the system of Reiki allows room for the client to find their own balance—to find what healing means for them. Reiki helps to bring the peace of mind for this balance to come. Sometimes that is all that is needed, and others it allows room and a foundation for the deeper, inner work of healing to begin.

I recommend that you try Reiki and see for yourself what changes it has on your life!

Ashwita's answer:

All the time, I have clients come to me who say something similar. They've tried it all, and many times this is just the last thing they are trying before they give up. And then the magic happens.

What makes Reiki different? The fact that there is no healer. A person who facilitates Reiki healing is often called a healer for the sake of simplicity, but this person does not do any healing at all, he or she merely facilitates – it is the energy that heals, that decides what needs to be done and how.

When the healer is a person, the healing is subject to various factors. The healer might not know enough or might miss taking something into consideration. And if they do, we know that even the best healers have bad days. Or the client might miss some important detail. And then there are times when the system can trick a healer, when the blocks move from one part of the body to another, creating an illusion of healing where nothing is really happening.

However, when we surrender to the energy itself and let it do whatever is required, not only do we see amazing results for the problem mentioned, but in many cases people report healing for issues they hadn't even mentioned or thought about. Reiki is really universal intelligence at play to help you heal, transform and transcend. I have not so far, encountered any system, which can match that.

Haripriya's answer:

Many of the tools that we use to heal ourselves are just tools. We may choose a spiritual approach or a scientific approach or a modality like Reiki that combines energy work with spirituality. None of these choices come with guarantees of any kind. It is completely up to us how we harness the power of the choices that we make to heal ourselves. Every system of healing offers something good and if we are open to it, it will teach us exactly what we need to learn at a given point on our life's path.

Miracles happen when we are equal participants in creating change, under the loving guidance of our Higher Self. Reiki shows us the path. It makes us aware of everything that is not serving us. It makes us aware of the self-sabotaging patterns that we carry. It opens our heart to love. It leads us to the doorway of light. But WE must make the choice to walk through this doorway.

And how can we accomplish this? By being regular with practice. By learning to flow with life rather than expect that our life must turn around overnight. By being wiling to work on everything that is not serving us well. No system fails us. The same holds true for Reiki too! If we are open to it, it works exactly as we need it to. It does not work the same way for everyone. And if we try to control the process of healing, it blocks the flow. The beauty of Reiki is that it puts the power right in our hands. And this is the most significant characteristic of the Reiki path towards healing.

Patti's answer:

Reiki is a healing modality developed in the 1900's by Mikao Usui. It is a Japanese hands on technique for stress reduction and relaxation that promotes the body's natural ability to heal itself. It is based on the idea that Life Force Energy flows through us all. If this energy is low or becomes blocked, stress or illness is more likely to occur. Conversely, if our energy is high we are more likely to feel good.

Reiki is not a fad. It has been around and working well for over a hundred years. It is not dependent on any religious belief, and has nothing to do with good or bad behavior. It is simply energy. Science confirms that all matter has energy. In the human body, energy runs along the spine through our chakra system.

Until you have experienced Reiki yourself, you may continue to question it. To eliminate doubt, my recommendation would be that you schedule a session with a local practitioner. Once you have felt the difference personally, you will come to see the immense value in this ancient practice.

I hope you continue to explore Reiki. If you take a Reiki class with a Reiki Master and become attuned, you will be able to feel healing energy in your own hands and transmit that to others. There are many gifts that come from being Reiki attuned, including a sense of calm and a fresh connection to nature. If your experience is anything like mine, you will see wonderful examples of healing from this simple, yet powerful gift.

Deb's answer:

Reiki is a unique energy healing modality, unlike any other scientific, spiritual or other modality. The Reiki practitioner is simply a channel for Universal Life Force Energy. This energy is guided by the Divine Consciousness, bringing healing to the physical, emotional/mental and/or spiritual aspects of a person's being. These loving energies are often directed to the root cause of an issue. While the resolution of a problem's symptoms may be the reason a person seeks Reiki treatments, and these symptoms may decrease or disappear, Reiki wisdom will also affect the underlying issues.

Let's explore some examples of this phenomenon. Judy scheduled a Reiki session to alleviate stress resulting in high levels of anxiety. Reiki helped her to relax and she easily fell into a deep meditative state. When the session ended, her first conscious thought was, "I need a new job!" This thought surprised her, as she felt secure and proud of her corporate position. Yet, she knew it was important to honor this thought, and she examined the benefits and costs of her current job in a realistic, in-depth way. She decided to be open to better possibilities, networked within her professional community and soon had a much more fulfilling, and less stressful, job. Her anxiety was gone.

Michael felt fatigued all day long, every day, and several friends urged him to try Reiki to boost his energy level. During the session, tears flowed as he finally allowed the grief he had stuffed inside over the past year. His father's death was the most difficult loss he had ever experienced. Although he was somewhat embarrassed by the emotional release, he noted his heavy heart felt much lighter. The compassionate Reiki practitioner provided loving reassurance, informing him the flow of tears was indeed an important healing moment for him.

When we open our hearts and souls to Spirit, healing is always available. Reiki is a beautiful modality, facilitating the healing process. Most often, healing occurs over a period of time, as a physical symptom or misguided belief is transformed – although miracles can, and do, happen within a session or two. Healing often manifests in unexpected ways. There are many possibilities as to why we may not be blessed with a physical cure, or a spiritual breakthrough. Perhaps, we are not ready to deal with a particular emotional issue; or, carrying a chronic condition may be part of our life plan and purpose. No matter what the result, Reiki always brings loving and healing energies into our lives.

Chapter 2 – Explaining Reiki

Question 2

How to explain Reiki to others?

Angie's answer:

The first thing to remember is that you aren't trying to convince them of anything or convert them! Sometimes our own enthusiasm, or fear that they won't understand, creates a problem where none exists. When someone who knows nothing about Reiki asks you about it, it is best to keep it very simple. You only need to share information—the basic facts—about what Reiki is. Base your response on how they asked the question, as this will let you know how much information they already have, how much they are interested in, and what they may be open to.

I tend to say something like this: "Reiki is a form of energy healing that helps the body and mind quickly return to their own natural state of balance so they can rest and heal. It's typically done through light touch on the body in several hand placements."

That is a very simple statement, yet it includes the pronunciation of Reiki (because I say the word), tells what it is, how it works, and how it is typically done. This is usually enough for most people to begin asking more questions, based on what they need to know. Their questions will guide you about what to say next. It's always a good idea to offer a demonstration. Many people are surprised to find out that they can feel the effects and benefits of Reiki in as little as 5 or 10 minutes. It's not a good idea to use words like "spiritual" or to over explain. Either of these things can scare people off. If they are interested in the spiritual aspects of Reiki, allow them to lead the way. It is perfectly valid to be interested in Reiki without being interested in that aspect of it.

Explaining distant Reiki can be a little trickier. Many people need an explanation of how the connection is made long distance without using a phone or computer. This is one of the most common questions I get. I usually remind them that our cell phones and Wi-Fi for our computers are connected through waves that we can't see. Though we are holding the device that the energy affects, the energy that connects the devices is invisible. All we can see is the result of the connection. It is the same with distant Reiki. We tune in to the energy of Reiki on our end, tune in to the person we are working with, and we send the intention of healing and balance through that connection. Not everyone will be able to accept this, but many will when they are able to make the connection to everyday devices like cell phones and Wi-Fi.

Question 3

How to explain distance healing to others?

What is the best way to explain how distance healing works to someone who has never experienced it?

Angie's answer:

I like to explain distant Reiki by relating it to the many other ways that we connect on a daily basis through methods of energy that we can't see.

We use methods such as Wi-Fi signals and cell phones each day and we think nothing of the fact that we can't see or even understand how the connection is made, even over thousands of miles and across the world. There are no wires or direct connections. It is all done through various types of energy. Energy has even allowed astronauts in space to communicate with people on Earth.

A hundred years ago this would have seemed ridiculous to most people, or possibly called evil. It wouldn't have been understood.

Now we know that there are many kinds of energy we can't see and we use many of them all the time. When we do distant Reiki, we are connecting to a form of energy that allows us to send healing, which could be viewed as a form of communication. Just as Wi-Fi might allow two people to connect across great distances via Skype or email, we connect via Reiki energy.

Question 4

How to explain Reiki to teenage children?

How to explain Reiki to teenage kids? They know their mum is doing Reiki, they sometimes ask for, but they still think that mum is doing "her things"...

Deb's answer:

Raising adolescents is certainly an exciting, and sometimes challenging, time. The fact your teenagers sometimes ask for Reiki is certainly exciting. Do they ask for Reiki for minor injuries, feelings of anxiety or sadness, or other reasons? You can expand their knowledge of how Reiki works by offering it for situations they have not yet considered. One example of this is to ask them to meditate with you while you send distance Reiki to the victims of a natural disaster. Adolescents often feel passionately about people who are dealing with tragic events, and they may appreciate participating in this way.

Because your teenagers have already experienced Reiki on a personal level, they must feel curious about the modality. Think about the personalities of your teenaged children. How do they like to learn? Do they like to read about a subject? Discuss a subject with parents or friends? Watch YouTube videos? Attend a seminar or workshop? There are many appealing and fun ways for them to learn more about Reiki.

Adolescence is such a special time in a person's life, as a young person vacillates between wanting to be treated as an adult some times, and acting like a child at other times. Reiki provides a great opportunity to introduce a grown-up way to approach the world. Someday, your children will leave your home and deal with this complex world. Reiki can become a wonderful tool to assist them throughout their adult years.

Chapter 3 – Hand Positions

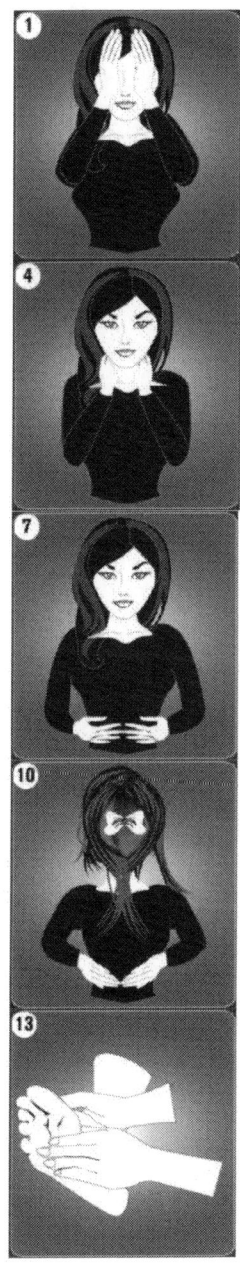
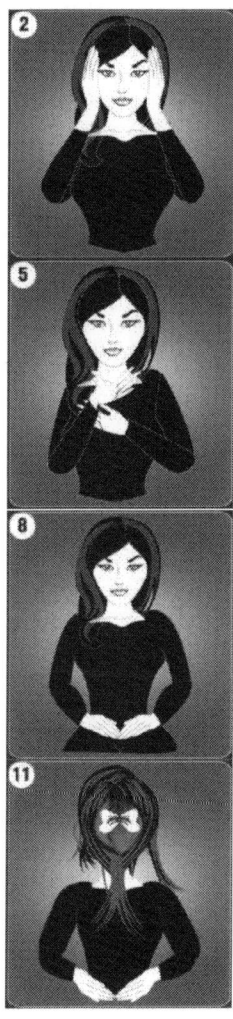
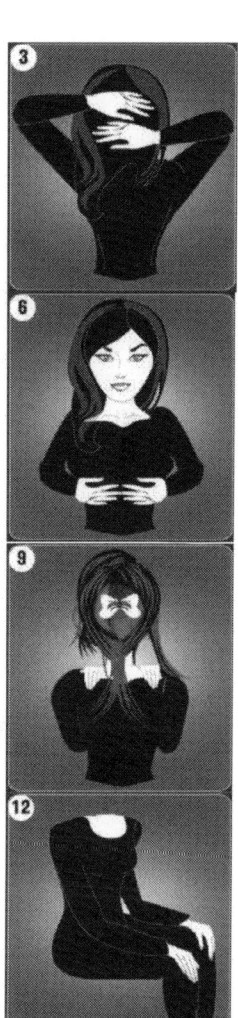

Reiki Hand Positions
for self-treatment
Reiki Rays © 2013
http://reikirays.com

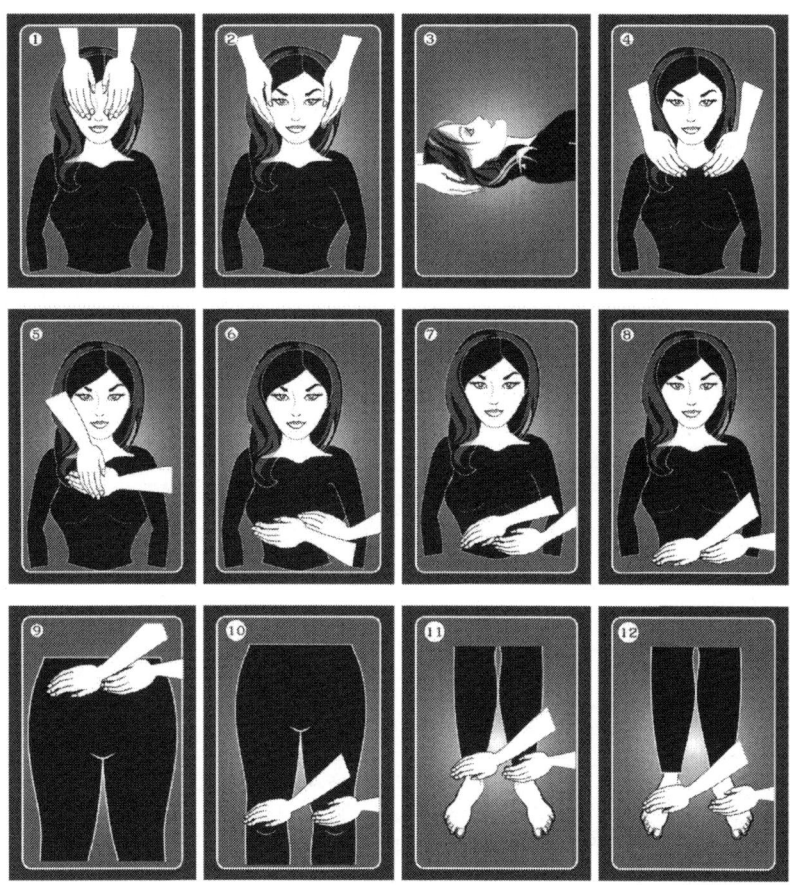

Reiki Hand Positions
for healing others
Reiki Rays © 2014
http://reikirays.com

Question 5

Why do we need hand positions?

If Reiki energy is able to reach where it is supposed to, why do hand positions exist?

Angie's answer:

When we say that Reiki goes where it needs to, the main meaning of that is that it will go to the root of any issues that need healing. It is because Reiki does this that we don't need to be able to do any kind of diagnostic work or have any intuitive capabilities. Reiki brings our system very quickly into its own state of rest and repair, allowing the energy to shift wherever it needs to for the highest good. This process means that a Reiki treatment can help bring balance to both the symptomatic issue and the root issue that caused it, even if it is unseen. That might mean you treat the head and something shifts in the foot, or you treat the liver and something shifts in the client's emotional life.

The hand positions are not meant to be rigidly clung to, but are used as guidelines. They closely follow the chakra system and the meridian system. Using the hand positions as a guideline to follow helps to ensure that the entire energy system is treated, thus supporting balance as fully as possible. However, if you have reason to focus on a particular area, such as pain or illness in that region, then it is certainly good to do so, as this will still help to bring about the rest and repair mode described above. Treating the head is almost always a good idea as this triggers this response very quickly, allowing the client to deeply rest, balance and heal.

Question 6

Is it necessary to go through all the hand positions when giving a Reiki treatment?

I work in a hospice as an assistant nurse and I sometimes have the opportunity to give the patients Reiki treatment but find it very difficult at times to do all the hand positions. I was wondering whether it is necessary to go through all the hand positions when giving a Reiki treatment?

Deb's answer:

Because Reiki's source is Universal Life Force Energy, the spiritual wisdom directs Reiki energies to wherever it is most helpful for the receiver. The ideal situation is to have at least one full hour available, have a massage table in a lovely, quiet treatment room, and be able to use all the hand positions. However, many times these elements are not possible. Reiki is still very effective. We can become comfortable in the knowledge that we are doing the best we can in any given situation.

For a hospice patient, any Reiki you give will be helpful – whether the Reiki goes to physical pain, maintaining calmness, or achieving acceptance of the dying process. You may be limited as to how much time you can spend on giving Reiki. Or, there may be physical limitations as you try to navigate around a hospital bed. Set your intention silently for the patient, and place your hands wherever you are able, and where you are guided. Reiki is always a beautiful gift; do not worry about the details. Reiki has no limits on the many ways it can bring compassionate healing and peace to a person who is in transition.

Question 7

How long should we send healing in each hand position and why?

Ashwita's answer:

The recommended duration for a beginner for each point is about 3 minutes. It is for this reason we commonly find Reiki music online with a gap of 3 minutes between bells, to indicate it is time to move to the next chakra.

The best duration for healing however is what your heart / body says. If you feel fluctuating sensations while healing, usually when the sensation rises and then falls, one 'cycle' of healing is over and you can move to the next point, or heal for another 'cycle'. If you find yourself (or your client) taking a deep breath, that is also often a sign that you can move to the next chakra.

The most powerful indicator for me is just the 'feeling' of having had enough. It takes some time and experience to get used to this, but once we are in touch with the feeling, it is quite easy. When healing a point, just ask yourself if it is enough. If you've received enough healing, it will feel OK to move. Otherwise, it feels very comforting to continue healing, and there is a hesitation in removing the hands. Once you get used to this method, you know you are quite deeply in touch with your body. There may be times you feel like healing a spot that isn't a traditional point, and you should follow this guidance.

Chapter 4 – Does Reiki Work

Question 8

How do I know if Reiki is working?

How do I know if Reiki is working? If some problem got fixed – was it on its own, or placebo, or was it actually Reiki?
Can I do Reiki on an inanimate object and prove to myself or others that it worked?

Ashwita's answer:

Usually if you are asking that question, it means that you don't really have faith in Reiki – and if it is still working for you, chances are very high that it is not placebo at all. Placebo would be if you strongly believed that Reiki would work, and it worked anyway.

Besides, why would we worry if it is placebo? It is just a medicine-biased mindset that wants proof for anything that is not yet attested in a lab. We know that up to 60% of the effects of pills could be placebo and that a sham surgery is as good as the real thing.** And yet, when we feel better after an aspirin or a surgery, we never ask the doctor if the healing was due to the real thing or because of placebo. Placebo is a very integral part of healing, and must be used to its best advantage.

It is a natural desire to want to see if Reiki works – we all want to test it to start believing in it more deeply. However, in my experience you cannot use Reiki just to prove something. It works when it works, and when you need it. There are instances where we can see it in action though.

Some of the ways one can try to experience the effect of Reiki is to:

- Heal someone who doesn't believe in Reiki but is genuinely open to try it out
- Heal an animal or a plant – both respond very quickly and positively

- Yes, heal an inanimate object. You can try healing your camera battery when it just goes down to the last stick. If you take the battery out and heal it for 10-15 minutes, the battery shows 2 sticks.

** Just in case you need a reference, here are two studies to support this statement:

http://journals.plos.org/plosone/article?id=10.1371/journal.pone.0015591 for pills
http://www.nejm.org/doi/full/10.1056/NEJMoa1305189 for surgery

Question 9

How can you tell, or know, that you are actually doing Reiki?

I know that once attuned, you practice and get better and better. But I try and practice, and seldom get any type of feedback from my self that the Reiki is actually flowing. I am not looking for any big "ta-da", but many say that they often get gentle signs, like warmth, tingle, etc., and I seldom get anything. I don't feel like anything has changed or improved. So I start to doubt and question and then have to reaffirm that I am "doing it right" – but how can you tell?

Patti's answer:

Reiki is accessing universal energy and allowing that energy to flow through our chakra system and out through our hands. The feeling of Reiki flowing differs somewhat from individual to individual but is generally characterized by a feeling of warmth or tingling in the hands.

Reiki energy is accessed through breath and intent. If you have been attuned and are calling in the energy in this manner, you can be assured that energy is flowing. Being properly grounded, using your strong breath and stating your intent clearly at the beginning of each session will ensure you have a solid connection to universal energy. Once you have practiced self-healing for some time, your flow will strengthen as your own energy blocks clear. With enough practice, energy will flow naturally and effortlessly. Let go of self-doubt, it is not your friend. Use affirmations such as "I am loving awareness" or "I radiate love and light and it reflects back to me."

You did not mention what level Reiki you are attuned to. Reiki I will have a much subtler feeling than a Reiki II or Reiki III/Master flow. I would encourage you to continue with your Reiki learning to expand your knowledge and enjoy the benefits of a stronger connection, and the increased confidence that education will bring. Join with other practitioners in your community or on line and enjoy support for your Reiki journey.

Question 10

How do you go about getting back into practicing Reiki after a break? How do you make it stronger and more effective?

I have my Reiki Master - but due to a lot of stuff happening in my life I have put it all on the back burner and not been able to concentrate on it. I know you don't lose it but how do you go about getting back into it and how do you make it stronger/more effective?

Patti's answer:

The answer to reclaiming your connection to energy is simply to practice. Get back to the basics of connecting to energy using your strong breath and clear intention. Take time to do this daily, even if just for a few minutes, and you will see noticeable improvement.

As you know, once attuned, always attuned. This does not mean however that our own energy does not get blocked by injury, stress or stagnation. Regular practice, self-healing and quiet meditation will go a long way toward restoring your strong flow; however, long periods of time without practice can leave you blocked energetically. You may want to assist the process by scheduling a cleansing energetic massage and / or a Reiki treatment from a fellow practitioner to move blocks along and out of your system.

Re-reading your Reiki manuals and other healing articles or books will refresh your knowledge and inspire you to continue with daily practice. Spending time with other healers in Reiki share groups will similarly assist in this.

Continue to learn and grow in your Reiki practice. This will increase your knowledge and open you to new healing methods. There are many courses available such as Shamanic Reiki, Purple and Violet Flame Reiki, Lightarian or Kundalini Reiki systems. Many of these include attunements. All of these will benefit and expand your practice.

Question 11

Does Reiki flow while having hands or legs crossed?

Some say that while giving and receiving Reiki hands / legs should not be crossed, while others I see give Reiki while sitting in lotus position. Is it ok to sit in lotus and give Reiki, or should we always give Reiki without our or clients' hands / legs crossed?

Ashwita's answer:

It is my experience that Reiki just does not flow if the legs are crossed, as we do while sitting on a chair. When healing clients, I have sometimes been surprised that Reiki doesn't seem to be flowing to them at all, only to realize that they had crossed their legs when I wasn't looking.

Crossing legs or arms is nature's way of helping us defend ourselves against perceived energy threats. While they are not tremendously effective, they do slow down the onslaught of unwelcome energy. However, sitting cross-legged on the floor (in the lotus or other yoga positions like siddhasana or sukhasana) does not offer this 'service'. On the contrary, it eases and facilitates a smooth flow of energy, which is why it is such a popular pose for meditation.

Reiki works just fine if one is sitting in the lotus pose. However, if one's legs are crossed at the knees or ankles while sitting in a chair or lying down, then Reiki tends to cease flowing.

Question 12

Can Reiki still flow when performing a healing session if the practitioner has carpal tunnel?

I am aware that Reiki is all about intention, and my heart tells me Yes – but still I thought I'd ask: Can Reiki still flow when performing a healing session if the practitioner has carpel tunnel?

Deb's answer:

Listen to your heart! This is your own intuitive wisdom speaking. Not only does Reiki flow to the receiver, when the practitioner has carpal tunnel syndrome or any other physical condition, Reiki will also bring healing energies to the practitioner. As the Reiki energies flow through the practitioner's Crown chakra, down through the other chakras and through the hands, it affects the practitioner's energy system. Giving Reiki to others benefits the practitioner's mind, body and spirit.

It is important, as a Reiki practitioner, to calm your mind and be open to the energies flowing through your own body during sessions. The intentions and mindfulness you bring into the treatment room will enable the client to feel more relaxed. Healing energies will flow with ease and grace. As you become more aligned with the Universal Life Force Energy, you become a more effective facilitator of healing for your client – and yourself. The benefits of Reiki are truly amazing.

Chapter 5 – Self Healing

Question 13

If you don't have much time to do Reiki, what are most important things that should be done?

Deb's answer:

With intention and daily practice, Reiki can become a vital part of every practitioner's life. It is not necessary to set aside an hour every day to do a full Reiki session. Rather, doing small amounts of Reiki throughout the day may be more meaningful.

Let me give you an example. When you awaken, greet the day with 10-15 minutes of Reiki self-treatment; an awareness of the many blessings in your life will increase. As you continue your day, send positive intentions to the commuters you meet, your colleagues and your work day. Complete your tasks, with the knowledge that Divine Wisdom exists within others and within yourself. Think frequently of Reiki and send loving energies to all people and situations in the world. If you have difficulties with coworkers, customers, friends or family members, send Reiki to them. Don't forget to give Reiki to yourself, a few minutes here and there. Remain calm and relaxed throughout the day and evening. End your day quietly with another 10-15 minutes of self-treatment; give gratitude for a day of blessings.

With daily practice, Reiki becomes a way of being and living – what a beautiful gift!

Question 14

Should you go through the entire process of calling the Reiki energy every time you are doing self-treatment?

Sometimes we do not have too much time available for self-healing, or we are really tired when we do it – for example, if we want to do a quick healing session while waiting for the elevator and we may only have 20 seconds available, or just before falling asleep when we are in bed after a long day.

Is it necessary for us to go through the entire process of calling in the Reiki energy every time we self-heal (and especially in situations such as the above), or is our intention enough?

Angie's answer:

If you set the intention for Reiki to flow, then you have actually already "called Reiki in."

There is no need to go through a long process each time. If you feel you need to do something more meditative or prayerful to help you feel connected to the energy, then that is fine, but having a set ritual is not required.

These things are simply ways to help us feel connected and for our minds to notice the shift in energy.

Question 15

If I do Reiki only once in a while, is it as effective (each time) as when it's done frequently?

I'm a Reiki practitioner. But with a busy life doing and being many things, I do not give Reiki or do self-Reiki that often. If I do Reiki only once in a while, is it as effective (each time) as it is when it's done frequently?

Angie's answer:

Reiki is beneficial each time it is done, no matter how long it has been since the last treatment. Every bit, no matter how small helps in some way. Reiki does have a cumulative effect, which means that it will continue to clear away blockages and heal more deeply each time it is done. However, it is still very effective when done only occasionally.

With sporadic treatments, you will get the benefit of pain reduction and stress reduction, which are pretty immediate. You will also get a short-term immune boost. With the cumulative effect, you will start to see overall improvements in your health, your emotional and mental wellbeing, your relationships and decision making. Your level of balance in life will seem to remain more stable. Recovery from stress will be easier. Either way, you receive wonderful benefits.

One thing I can recommend is doing shorter, but more frequent sessions on a daily basis. Even 5 or 10 minutes will bring the cumulative results of Reiki. It is usually possible to fit such a short amount of time into the day, even if it is only as you are falling asleep. However, if it is simply not possible, then do Reiki whenever you can and you will still receive much benefit from it, including pain and stress reduction, and boosting your immune system.

Question 16

Why am I falling asleep during self-healing sessions?

I noticed that when I'm giving Reiki to myself, I often doze off. I would like to know why this happens, and how do I overcome this. Thank you.

Deb's answer:

I often have clients fall asleep during Reiki treatment sessions. I like to use Reiki for myself, at the end of my days. Like most people, I have a busy life and sometimes it is hard for me to turn off my thoughts and fall asleep peacefully. I find using Reiki at bedtime calms me, and I get a better night's sleep when I am connected with the Universal energies.

I do not think your dosing off is something to overcome. I wonder if you might be worrying that Reiki is not working in your self-treatments, because you are no longer able to intentionally place your hands in certain positions. However, the Universe is aware of your initial intentions and will continue to work, even if you fall asleep. In fact, the Universe may have wanted you to fall sleep.

Whenever someone falls asleep during Reiki treatments, I view this as the physical body needing that kind of peaceful rest. Also, I think specific energies focused on particular physical benefits may need the body to be at total rest to be most effective. The sleeping body will accept these energies more easily, and physical healing will happen at a faster pace.

Restful sleep is always restorative. Combining that kind of sleep, with the healing and loving energies of Reiki, is a great way to achieve a true balance of mind, body and spirit healing.

Reiki always heals. In your case, it is likely sleep is an important ingredient for your healing to occur.

Angie's answer:

It is actually OK to become very relaxed and fall asleep while you are doing Reiki self-treatment. It is very normal for anyone receiving Reiki to become very relaxed and many become sleepy and drift off. It's no different when you are receiving Reiki directly. Open your self-treatment session by asking to be an open channel for Reiki to flow into you for the greatest and highest good. Then rest in the knowledge that you are being supported in the best possible manner during and after the session. If that includes sleep, then that may be what is best for you in that moment. Don't worry about changing hand positions; remember the Reiki is intelligent and will flow where it is needed.

If you self-treat at a time of day when you need to stay awake, such as in the morning before work, then consider setting an alarm so that you won't be late if you fall asleep during Reiki. You might also consider doing your treatment at another time of day when falling asleep won't matter very much to your schedule. Another option you could consider is to treat yourself while sitting up, or while following a video with prompts.

Question 17

I practice self-healing daily. Why do I still get sick?

I practice Reiki daily, and there are days in which I practice twice. Yet I have discovered that I have ovarian cysts which are causing much pain; so where I was wrong?
Why do seasoned healers with lots of years of daily self-healing under their belt get sick?

Deb's answer:

When a Reiki practitioner has medical issues, it is no reflection on whether or not the practitioner practices Reiki correctly. There are many reasons why everyone has, or will have, problems within their physical bodies during their lives. Our bodies are simply vehicles for our spiritual selves, and they are not designed to live forever. In fact, our bodies are complicated, complex mechanisms with many working parts. Everything affects these working parts. We cannot overestimate the energies our bodies absorb from other people in our lives, the foods and drinks we ingest, to the local and global environment in which we live, to the thoughts we have and words we say, every minute of our lives. Embracing Reiki builds our awareness of this reality.

It may be helpful to have a Reiki session with another Reiki practitioner. Often, other healing practitioners will receive impressions or messages about your energy field that you are unable to access. It can be difficult to receive information about ourselves from an objective point of view. Another person may intuit what is happening in our energetic fields as she "feels" the energy from a more detached place. This level of compassionate neutrality creates openness and distance from the problem. In other words, as a client, you may gain understanding as to the cause of these cysts, why you may not be ready to release them from your physical self, or the purpose of them in your own soul growth.

Remember – Reiki always heals but does not guarantee that we will never experience physical, emotional or spiritual issues. In fact, these issues may be blessings, coming into our lives to help us grow.

Patti's answer:

As much as we would like to believe differently, we healers are human, and therefore subject to the same illnesses as other people. We are not impervious to germs from sharing tight space in a plane or flu sickness that runs through our family. As humans, we also respond emotionally to events that happen in the world or to people we know and love. I believe the strength of our immunity has a direct correlation to these factors: a healthy diet, maintenance of our spiritual and emotional condition with exercise and meditation, and our regular practice of self-healing.

As healers, we typically have better resistance to illness and negativity than the general public, however our energy is not static. Energy shifts in response to solar and lunar cycles, emotions and life circumstances. Sometimes illness in the body is a reflection of what is going on in our personal lives. If you are experiencing symptoms, ask yourself what the deeper meaning may be. Is there a problem area in your life or relationships that should be addressed?
Familiarity with herbal remedies and essential oils that can lessen symptoms and speed recovery. Additional support in the form of yoga, massage, chiropractic care or other healthy activities helps to keep us feeling our best.

Question 18

What to do when you get sick as a Reiki Master?

What do you do when you get sick as a Reiki Master? I find it very difficult to do self-treatment when sick.

Angie's answer:

When we get sick, it can feel as if our treatment isn't doing any good, or as if it is blocked altogether. It is still a good idea to do what you can. If you are feeling too ill to place your hands in the hand positions, don't concern yourself with that. Simply call in Reiki and know that it is working. You can use visualization to help you move Reiki through your system to the places where you feel the most in need. This can be very empowering. For this reason, guided meditations and visualizations that work with violet light or with Reiki can be very healing during illness.

Remember to charge you food, water, tea and medications with Reiki, as this gives you an extra boost. Also, don't hesitate to seek treatment from another practitioner when you are ill! This is often a very good idea and it can help get your energy channels open and balanced more quickly.

Question 19

What is the best way to heal yourself using Reiki if you have anxiety / panic attacks?

Ashwita's answer:

The opposite of anxiety or panic is relaxation. But most of the times, we want to relax in the absence of the anxiety and this creates further stress in the system as we are trying to fight the anxiety. Change that approach – relax into the anxiety.

So, the first step would be don't panic that you are having a panic attack. Often it is not what we are going through, but our fears and resistance to what is happening, that worsen the situation greatly. So to start working with it more deeply, always start by checking if you are resisting the panic or anxiety attack, and remind yourself that it is ok for this to happen.

Start to become more and more aware of the parts of your body that are having any sensations – could be your heart, feet, solar plexus, or any part of the body. Now join your fingertips, and draw Sei He Ki and Cho Ku Rei (if you have learned level 2, otherwise this step can be skipped) in your heart or Solar Plexus – wherever it feels right, and request Reiki to bring you in deeper touch with your body and the sensations. Don't try to 'fix' the sensations, merely feel them. If you feel too much out of control, you can also breathe deeply, powerfully and rapidly for about a minute while joining your fingertips, and then tune in to your body.

Once the bodily sensations start to fade automatically, place your hands on the areas that still have any sensations left, or on the heart or solar plexus. Draw all the symbols in the heart or solar plexus a few times, requesting Reiki to release any remaining stress in the body.

Chapter 6 – Symbols

Question 20

If Reiki is universal healing energy, why do we need special symbols or an attunement process to open ourselves up to this flow?

I am a big fan of Reiki Rays and it came to me at a very opportune moment in my life, almost re-introducing me to Reiki, which I had abandoned ten years ago. Reiki is now a big part of my life. However, my logical brain keeps pestering me with this question: If Reiki is universal healing energy, why do we need special symbols or an attunement process to open ourselves up to this flow?

Angie's answer:

First, thank you for your kind words about our work at Reiki Rays. I'm very glad the site came to you at just the right time.

You have asked an excellent question. Reiki is indeed Universal Healing Energy and it is available to all of us. We have it within us and it is all around us. We have simply "forgotten" on a conscious level that it is there. However, that forgetting is a big issue for most people.

If we were to set the intention to focus on reacquainting ourselves with our own energy and the life force energy all around us, making this a primary goal in our lives to tune in, we would redevelop this in time. We would need to heal all of the blocks we had built up over the years that had kept us from believing that such energy existed and that we could access it—a big layer of blocks for many people! It can take a lot to even get to the point that we can see what we need to do to begin. It is always the healing of ourselves that must be accomplished first.

There are many methods, in many different systems of achieving self-growth and understanding energy. Most employ some form of meditation and self-reflection. Most see the importance of honoring our connection with each other and all things and intentionally seeking to feel that connection regularly, through ritual, prayer, communion or some other means. The trouble is, it can take many years, or even a lifetime of practice for some to really begin to feel a connection in a deep way. Of course, the more dedicated to the practices and to the connection, the easier it will come in most cases, but that isn't always true. For some it is simply very difficult, no matter how dedicated they are. Reiki attunement is a very deep healing that begins to clear away the blocks that prevent connection. For those who want to work very deeply on their healing and want to deeply understand their connection to Universal Energy, this is an expedient means to achieve that. However, it doesn't eliminate the need for intentional connection, dedication and finding ways to connect. Mikao Usui taught meditations and praying the Reiki principles as a means to assist in this.

As for the symbols – we don't need the symbols. No practitioner needs the symbols. It is entirely possible and very effective to heal and even to connect distantly without using the symbols. However, the symbols are tools, in much the same way the attunement is a tool. They help us to connect to particular aspects of the energy. They represent something that is energy. Actually, everything represents something that is energy, including the words you are reading right now. And the thoughts and emotions you are having about the words you are reading. Even our bodies represent something that is actually energy. The symbols are specific vibrations of energy, much the way a note played on an instrument is a specific vibration of energy. The instrument can be played without tuning in to each note that is possible, but each note that is struck enriches the musical experience. So it is with symbols and Reiki.

Question 21

Are the symbols manipulating the Reiki energy?

We are always told that you should not try to manipulate Reiki; just let it flow and it will do the highest good. That being the case, aren't the symbols manipulating the Reiki? If Reiki is an intelligent energy that always does what is most needed what's the point in the symbols?

Haripriya's answer:

The Reiki symbols are not something non-Reiki. They are energy signatures of Reiki. They are in tune with the energetic frequency of Reiki energy and work in harmony with it.

Using the symbols does not mean that we are manipulating the energy. Just like we turn on switches to use electrical energy for varied purposes, we use the Reiki symbols to focus Reiki energy for different healing purposes. In short, working with the Reiki symbols is the same as working with Reiki.

Question 22

Is it necessary to draw the symbols on your palms and on your client?

Everyone approaches Reiki differently. I have always drawn my symbols, but am wondering if it is actually necessary to draw them on your palms and on your client?

Haripriya's answer:

In the early stages of one's practice, it is always a good idea to draw the symbols frequently. However, as we practice and especially if we are regular with practice, the energy of the symbols gets deeply embedded in our energy fields and becomes part of us. So, we may not find it essential to draw the symbols every time – on our palms or on clients.

However, if we are intuitively guided to draw a specific symbol at any point during practice or treatments, it is good to do so. Sometimes drawing a symbol adds additional power to healing sessions. Our intuition is our best guide. Trusting the power of our intuition will help us know exactly when we would benefit by drawing the symbols.

Question 23

Can you use some symbols without initiation?

If you have to be initiated into the symbols for Reiki, how is it that you can use other symbols without initiation?

Haripriya's answer:

This is in keeping with the widely accepted Reiki tradition, wherein the Reiki Master acts as an instrument to awaken another's ability to consciously channel Reiki. The Reiki attunement serves to strengthen the student's innate connection with the energy. The symbols are nothing but energy signatures that resonate with the energy frequency of Reiki. Therefore, when we use the symbols after a Reiki attunement, we find that we are able to use them more powerfully than if we used them without an attunement.

Chapter 7 – Distance Healing

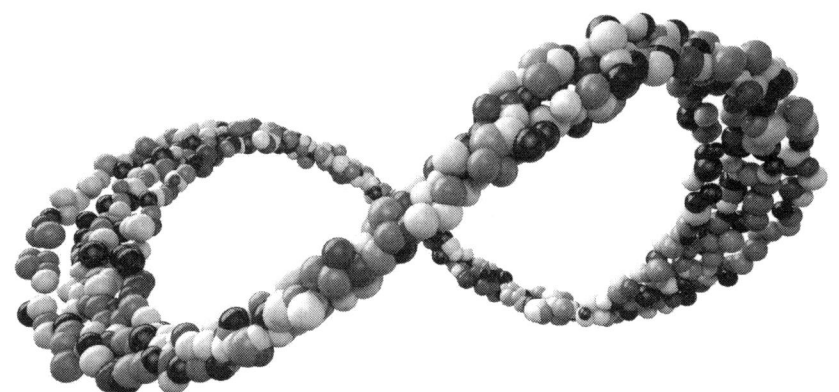

Question 24

How to proceed when someone on Facebook asks for a healing?

How do you proceed when someone on Facebook asks for a healing? If there is a big demand do you send it to the group or individually? And how long should it last?

Patti's answer:

There are a couple of points to address here. A Facebook request for healing can be quite general, as in the case of a post calling for healing for a relative or friend in physical or emotional crisis. These requests are sent to everyone who sees the post. For a general request for healing, it is fine to simply send healing right away, when you see the request, knowing that others who see the request will be sending healing also. Alternatively, if you set aside a daily meditation time, you can send healing in response to the group or individual, as well as any other situations you are aware of that need healing. For general requests, it is nice to know that you are not the only healer involved. In this circumstance, we join with other like-minded individuals for the common good and send light and love into the world and to specific events. Sit quietly with your intention and let the energy flow for as long as you'd like. However long you spend in this meditative state, you will do much good!

For requests that are specifically directed to you, schedule an agreed upon time with the recipient. Determine in advance if you will charge a fee for your service and if so, use your normal rate for a 30 minute or 60-minute session. When done in this manner, you will be able to set aside the proper amount of time for your session, ensure that the receiver is in a place where they can relax and fully integrate the healing energy, and that they get the time they have paid for. A distance healing session should follow the same format as a healing session performed in person.

Question 25

How does Reiki find its way to someone who gives just an initial?

How does Reiki find its way to those who just give an initial of their name when requesting distant healing? How effective is the healing that is being sent? How long do we spend on sending?

Haripriya's answer:

By virtue of being an intelligent energy, Reiki knows how exactly to reach someone who intends to receive it. While we may not understand how exactly this occurs from a scientific perspective, all experienced practitioners know that Reiki is not bound by space, time or any other physical restrictions. We are all energetically connected and energy flows where we intend it to.

Distance healing is as effective as healing in person. There are no hard and fast rules as to the duration. The best option is to offer a distance healing exactly like an in person healing. So, if your average in person healing session lasts 45 to 60 minutes approximately, the same would be true for a distance healing as well.

Question 26

Are the intuitions I get during distance Reiki healing sessions true?

During my Distance Reiki healing sessions, I get visions or intuitions. Sometimes these turn out to be absolutely accurate and other times there seems to be no connection to the person I am healing. Are these intuitions true or are they a figment of my overactive imagination?

Ashwita's answer:

If you have intuitive abilities, you start to see things about a person while healing them. Some of this information will be from the physical realm, and will be easy to relate to. However, we sometimes receive information from other realms or dimensions as well and sometimes this might make no sense at all. Sometimes on talking about it, you realize you might have accessed a past life and the consequences of such an event are still visible in their lives (for example, a woman who I saw being sexually assaulted in a previous life later said she had issues with intimacy despite having no reason to be frigid, confusing her very loving partner).

In my experience, having visions is only one of the side effects of healing getting deeper, and can be a trap if one gets involved. If you try not paying much attention to the visions you see and leaving the healing truly to the universe, you might find that you are able to facilitate healing deeper than you ever imagined.

Question 27

Is there some way to "compress" time and do what would be a 60 minutes healing session in less time?

In distance healing, I have seen offerings for 30 minutes sessions and 60 minutes sessions. I've heard that 15 minutes of Reiki will be good for an hour distance session. What would you do if you were to give a client a 30 minutes distance Reiki session? Is it still the same as in a 60 minutes distance session?

Deb's answer:

It is very disappointing that someone told you 15 minutes of Reiki would be sufficient for an hour of distance healing. We cannot offer a 30-minute or 60-minute Reiki session and then give Reiki for fewer minutes than what we offered. Our work must match the fees received from a client. If there is a legitimate reason why a practitioner can only do 15 minutes of Reiki, then she should only charge for 15 minutes of Reiki. This applies to both in-person sessions and distance healing sessions.

Anyone who provides a service must develop trust and integrity with his clients. Authenticity and honesty are essential in establishing our Reiki practices. In complementary energy healing practices, we must be diligent in maintaining integrity, as there is still skepticism surrounding our work. We must do everything we can to develop a respected name for ourselves, for Reiki, and for all alternative treatment practitioners.

Question 28

Does healing work when receiving Reiki on YouTube?

People take videos sending healing on YouTube. Does it really work? When you watch does it heal you? Is it effective?

Ashwita's answer:

Reiki heals through intent. However, for an intention to be strong enough, one has to have a strong enough practice, and also for sufficient duration. So if a level 1 Reiki healer who hasn't had any other spiritual practice and has only just learned Reiki made a video to send healing, I would doubt the effectiveness of that. On the other hand, if a person has a few years of earnest Reiki practice behind them and genuinely intends to send healing to everyone who watches the video, then that can be quite miraculous.

The most important factor therefore – honesty – remains a question-mark, and one needs to trust one's own heart while watching such a video. However, to answer your question in short, yes, it can work and yes it can heal you.

Chapter 8 – Attunements

Question 29

Does one get any indication of the flow of energy after an attunement?

After the attunement, how does one know that she / he has now got the power to heal? Does one get any indication of the flow of energy?

Angie's answer:

The flow of energy can often be very subtle. For some, it may feel very intense at first and then gradually settle down. But for others, the flow feels subtle and it takes practice and regular self-healing to begin to notice it and feel confident in what they are feeling.

Doing daily self-healing will bring a stronger awareness of the flow of energy over time. You will tune in to the flow as you work with Reiki each day, so you will become more familiar with it and with how it shifts and changes. You will also start to see the healing working within you, which will confirm to you that the attunement has worked. You need to practice with Reiki regularly in order to increase your awareness of it. Use it in many ways in your everyday life to get lots of benefit from it and to increase your understanding.

It is like any other tool—the more you use it, the better you understand how it works and the more competent you feel with it. It can also help to keep a journal to record how you feel and a few specifics of how your life is going for the first few months after you are attuned and begin self-Reiki practice. This can give you a record of the subtle changes that occur that can be more difficult to see on a daily basis.

Question 30

How can I know for sure if the remote attunement was really performed?

I have received a remote attunement. My question is: how can I know for sure if the attunement was really performed and I am attuned?

Patti's answer:

For remote attunement, you must be confident that you are dealing with a reputable teacher. Do your homework. Check reviews and speak to the teacher on the phone to ensure you both agree on what you are getting for the price you pay. A good teacher will make sure that you feel comfortable with their sincerity. They will be happy to have a conversation with you to help you feel assured they will follow through appropriately.

Remote attunement will usually involve setting a time to "meet". Once you have scheduled and completed your remote attunement with a trusted Master, you can be certain that you are indeed attuned. Be sure to take some time to relax after the attunement and allow the new energy to integrate. If possible, check in with your teacher and share any experiences in regard to the attunement.

Question 31

What is the right way to attune a student and what role does intuition play in the attunement process?

I have found that the attunement is different from teacher to teacher. I have so many different books and so many different ways taught as well as what I was taught. My teacher gave us both the traditional and Tibetan Master Symbol, which despite their good intention, has created more confusion.
There seems to be so much controversy with Reiki.
So what is the right way to attune a student? Is it true that each teacher is guided to attune by their own intuition and inner Reiki guidance? How have others dealt with all this controversy?

Angie's answer:

When a Reiki Master teaches that there are a variety of ways to attune a student and that you have to follow your own guidance, they are correct. There are basic guidelines, but there can be variations even from one student to the next, based on the energy. Even the original teachers didn't always teach Reiki or attune the same way and their styles differed from each other. There is much evidence of this now. The understanding of adjusting to the student, the energy and your own guidance comes with doing attunements and with time. The intention is the most important thing, followed by the basic outline of placing the symbols that represent the Reiki energy into the student to begin opening their channels and allowing Reiki to flow. Though you will read variations in how to do this, or perhaps slight variations in the order or even which symbols to use, the basic outline of the attunement process is essentially the same everywhere. If your energy is in the correct state, you set the intention to do an attunement to a specific level, and follow the basic outline, the attunement should work fine. Practice this and your discomfort should diminish quickly.

Do not worry about the symbols that your Reiki Master taught you. Both the Master symbols are valid, as they represent the same energy. Use whichever one resonates with you the most, as that will likely be the one that will work the best for you. Symbols are not power, in and of themselves. They are representations of energy forms, or energy states. Symbols are not necessary for Reiki to work; they are only tools. Use the tools that work best for you and leave the rest.

If you felt your teacher was competent and you felt the attunement you had was valid, then perhaps you can explore how you feel for a while and consider letting go of any controversy and the opinions of others. Give yourself Reiki, above all. And offer Reiki to the situation, asking it to guide you to what is right for you. Remember that Reiki is Universal Life Force energy. No one owns Reiki. No one person gets to decide how Reiki will be experienced by all people. No one can truly describe Reiki, though many insist they can. We each have our own relationship with it. Explore yours. I wish you well.

Question 32

Should Reiki be completed in the one lineage?

What are your thoughts regarding accepting people to do Reiki II if Reiki I is completed with someone else?
Should Reiki be completed in the one lineage?

Angie's answer:

I think it is fine to accept someone who has completed level 1 with another teacher. It is a good idea to talk to the student and be sure that your ideas about Reiki are in alignment with theirs prior to having them sign up for the class, but if you feel like you are a match with each other, then I see no problem with that at all. Reiki is Universal. There is no need to restrict ourselves to one lineage. Students need to find the teacher they feel most comfortable with and teachers need to teach students they feel are best suited for the way they teach.

There can actually be a lot of benefit to having different teachers, as it offers you different perspectives on Reiki, as well as on teaching. For the teacher, seeing students from different teachers does the same thing. We can all learn something from each other, if we remain open to it.

Question 33

What is the earliest age that a person can be attuned to Reiki?

Ashwita's answer:

It depends. Normally there is no need for attunement before the age of 7 or 8. Many parents who have learned Reiki from me eventually share stories of how their children learned to practice Reiki by just watching them, and how they are now more effective healers. I usually suggest an attunement around 7-8 years of age if the child is interested.

There may be some exceptions in rare cases, but that is up to the Reiki teacher to decide. I once attuned a 3-month old fetus, and it was only when I was done with it, that I remembered that I never suggest attunements before 7-8. I was working intuitively and had no idea why I had done what I did. We now know that the child was conceived in difficult circumstances and probably had very low energy. If a child is facing very difficult circumstances, it may be a good idea to ask a teacher if an attunement is required. Normally it is not.

Question 34

How do I start attuning others and what are the ways to give attunements to students?

I'm nervous about teaching Reiki and giving attunements to students. How do I start and what are the ways to give attunement to students?

Haripriya's answer:

You can start off by attuning people who are already attuned. Practice brings confidence. Practicing on someone who is already attuned can help you relax, as you will not need to worry about offering a perfect attunement. Once you have practiced sufficiently and are fairly confident, you can begin to offer attunements to interested people in your own circle of friends and family. This will help you grow in confidence and help you take the next step of offering attunements to students. To give an attunement, you will need to follow the step by step procedure that your own teacher taught you. However, do feel free to trust your intuition while offering attunements. In case you spontaneously feel like adding an additional step or two, trust the voice that is guiding you and go ahead with confidence.

Question 35

Is it possible to be attuned by video? Does it work?

Patti's answer:

It is possible to be attuned by video, as there are no time space limitations with energy. However, attunement can be a very personal process between a student and a Reiki master. You will want to select your attunement process based on your available resources, factoring in what you have available for time and expenses.

Forms of attunement range from one-on-one contact in person, to distance by phone or computer, to remote attunements scheduled in real time and of course, as you mentioned, video attunements that are available on line or via media any time. Any of the above will work, but there is great value in personal contact and continuing mentorship.

When exploring attunement options, make sure you are getting what you pay for. Find out what is available in your local area for the modality you want, then choose the most effective attunement process for your needs.

Question 36

What are the advantages / disadvantages of being attuned in one Reiki type over another?

There are different types of Reiki but what are the advantages / disadvantages of being attuned in one type over another? I have heard of classes being taught in Usui, Karuna®, Soma. I know Usui is the original type of Reiki. But some of the others are pretty interesting as well. Just curious. And thank you!

Ashwita's answer:

There are more than 750 different types of Reiki (that I know of) available today, with every other teacher customizing it for specific areas of life – more money, finding life-partners, etc., and also other teachers tuning in to specific streams of energy, like dolphin energy, whale energy, energy of the moon, etc. Others are lineage specific, or idea specific, for example Karuna® Reiki taps into compassion.

For the sake of understanding, let use the analogy of watering a plant to explain healing oneself through Reiki. Ultimately, what the plant needs is water, everyday – your daily self-healing practice. Now, water is water – energy is energy, even more so if we are tuning in to universal energy, which is what 'Reiki' roughly translates to.

Now, you can make a variety of waters. Some maybe enriched with some nutrition that plants might require, some might contain additives that might specifically help with more rose flowers, some stronger roots, some might have antibiotics to remove disease, etc. Other waters might be location specific, like water from a sacred river, mountain streams, a specific sea, etc. Ultimately, it is all just water. But sometimes, we might want another 'variety'.

The thing is, once you truly tune in to Reiki, it will bring you everything you need. But it is the age of shortcuts and we all want things fast, so it is quite lucrative to try out a few different types of Reiki. Ultimately, it is very important to remember that it is the watering that is most important. You can give tap water or nutritious water, but if you forget to water, the plant will suffer and it will take a lot more than watering to bring it back to life. So no matter what, keep up that daily practice!

Question 37

Why can't I use Karuna® Reiki if I'm attuned to Usui Reiki?

If Reiki Energy is a Universal Energy and I am attuned to Usui Reiki, then why is it said that I cannot use Karuna® Reiki or its symbols, or vice versa?

Patti's answer:

I love this question! One of my favorite things about Reiki is that there are so many variations available for us to learn and benefit from. There is nothing quite like learning a new style of Reiki and feeling new, powerful energy surround and flow in and through you. Learning a new modality not only increases access to energy flow, it allows us to more deeply align with Spirit and nature, thereby strengthening our intuition.

Each system of Reiki has its particular band of vibrational frequency and we are attuned to each specific band depending on which system of Reiki we study. Karuna® Reiki has a different frequency than Usui Reiki, as does Kundalini, Lightarian Reiki, Violet Flame and others. Each version of Reiki requires an attunement, sometimes multiple attunements, that open the pathway to allow access to the specific bands of energy. Often, symbols accompany the attunements and are passed down by the Reiki Master. These are used in certain treatments, such as emotional or distance healing as well as the master symbols used by teachers to attune students. Though you may find access to a certain symbol in a book or on line, until you are attuned to it, you will have little or no success in using it.

Attunements to different bands of vibrations associated with each system of Reiki should be taken over time. Just as you are instructed to wait between attunements of Reiki I, II and III, you will want to span your Reiki training over a period of months, or even years. This will allow you to be fully integrated with the energy of one system of Reiki before you pursue the next. Practice with the individual benefits of each system and increase your knowledge as you are guided by your Reiki Master and spirit guides.

Chapter 9 – Reiki Practice

Question 38

How do I know when I am ready and able to provide Reiki healing sessions on others?

Patti's answer:

Once you are attuned to Reiki I, you are ready to begin self healing and to practice on family members, friends and pets. After being attuned to Reiki II, you should be fully prepared to provide healing sessions to the public for a fee or on a volunteer basis.

Reiki I training should include materials describing the origins and history of Reiki, instruction concerning hand placement for Reiki treatments, and the Reiki I attunement. Reiki II is a bit more in depth and should include a written handout, instruction on the Reiki II symbols, and the Reiki II attunement. A waiting period of 21 days or longer to allow the energy to fully integrate is recommended between the Reiki I and Reiki II attunements. Self healing should be practiced daily during this time.

Reiki is intuitive energy. Whatever level you are at, if you have been attuned by a qualified Reiki Master, you can be confident that the energy will flow when accessed with breath and intent.

Question 39

How do I get over my insecurity regarding offering Reiki?

How do I get over my insecurity so that I can offer Reiki to others and do more than just use it quietly on myself?

Haripriya's answer:

By becoming aware that Reiki is Universal Life Force energy. It is not a skill that must be mastered before it is offered to others. It is loving energy that is the heart beat of the Universe. It is the energy that keeps us alive. It is very close to us, even if we are not conscious of it. When we open ourselves to Reiki, it flows through us in perfect harmony and reaches others in the way that they need it. We do not have to direct its flow. All we need to do is allow it to flow and the rest will be taken care of. This awareness can make you feel secure and confident about offering Reiki to others.

Question 40

Do I always need to be in a certain frame of mind to perform Reiki?

Do I always need to be in a certain frame of mind to perform Reiki? Sometimes I don't feel a connection with the universe or spirits and I don't feel like it worked for the other person. What's going on?

Patti's answer:

We need always be vigilant in our attitude when connecting to energy to treat others. If it is in your practice, use a special ritual to call in your spirit guides and ancestors. Draw a Reiki power symbol on each of the walls to prepare the treatment area. Add any other symbols you feel called to use while creating sacred space.

We prepare ourselves mentally by taking the time to connect to our guides and clear ourselves of the things that stress us in our daily living. Commit fully to this process and trust universal energy to respond. Once we have sincerely taken these steps, we can be assured that healing energy will flow to the recipient and we can release any self-doubt.

Even though we are healers, we are still human. Our feelings will vary depending on what our day looks like. Also, our perception of the session may vary substantially from the receiver's. Even if you are feeling that the energy is less than desired, the recipient may have a totally different reaction, often having a powerful healing experience.

Question 41

What should I be thinking or saying inside my head while I give a Reiki session?

Sometimes I am not sure what I should be thinking or saying inside my head while I give a Reiki session. Depending on the person and what they need I usually address it but I usually just repeat the 4 symbols and ask to fill the client with white light and remove any negative energies. Do you have any recommendation on what else should I be saying or thinking?

Ashwita's answer:

You seem to be doing just fine. What I love about Reiki is that it does not have any specific direction – the main objective is balance of the energy system, and that is a wonderful thing to ask for. You don't even have to ask this in words – before you begin a healing, request Reiki to bring you into balance, and the rest will happen automatically.

I would avoid asking Reiki to remove 'any negative energies', because we need a balance of positive and negative energies to be healthy and happy. Without any negative energies, our excretory system would not work. Electricity is also nothing but negative energy – purely electrons, and look how it lights up our lives! I ask Reiki to balance instead of charge someone positively, as I have observed that balance brings far greater and longer-lasting stability to their energies. Try it and see if you resonate with it too.

As for saying or thinking something during a session, I believe that the lesser said, the better. The mind can be an obstacle more often than not, and I prefer letting the energy decide what's best. This can facilitate much deeper healing. It is common for a client to come for a minor problem and have a much more serious problem get detected and healed or get appropriate medical attention within just a few days, and the minor problem might have remained completely untouched. I prefer it that way.

We talk all the time about using Reiki, but isn't it so much better to let Reiki use us? When you invoke Reiki, ask it to use you as a channel in the best way possible, and surrender yourself to the force. Healings become much, much deeper because through this, we really set the ego aside and trust the energy to do its thing. Thoughts might come and go, don't pay them much heed. Many times people might even pick up information about the client or areas where the blocks are, but I have found that when I just let those thoughts be, instead of rushing to 'fix' them, healing happens much faster and is much deeper.

Question 42

How do you keep your mind focused on treating your client during your Reiki sessions?

Angie's answer:

The mind naturally wants to busy itself when it is not active. It is the normal state for the mind to be in. One reason having a regular meditation practice is so helpful is that we learn to understand that it is normal for the mind to want to fidget, and we also learn to let go of the fidgeting. We can see what comes up in our mind, acknowledge it and release it without becoming involved in it or attached to it. This helps us to focus our mind on one thing and to allow it to be open to whatever arises, without becoming so reactive and judgmental — most of the time.

The best way to help yourself focus during client Reiki sessions is to develop a meditation practice and bring elements of that into your session. Your meditation practice can be very simple and it doesn't need to be long. The goal is to implement the practice for at least a few minutes each day to help your mind learn the new skill. One of the simplest methods of meditation is to place your focus on your breath, without changing your breathing. Your attention will drift, which is normal, but when it does, gently guide it back to your breath.

You can apply this same technique to a client session, placing your attention on your breath, with gentle attention on your client as you work. Reiki will do its work without a great effort on your part, so this meditative practice is all that is needed to keep the energy open and your focus in the situation.

Question 43

Do you work on the body 'system' where the dis-ease started, or do you just treat as a whole?

If a client is faced with any dis-ease ranging from Eczema to Period Pains to Heart Disease and Cancer, what is the best approach? Do you work on the body 'system' where the dis-ease started, or do you just treat as a whole?

Haripriya's answer:

We generally treat the system as a whole. The basic premise is that any kind of an imbalance (including physical disease) occurs because of a disharmony in the flow of energy within and around our bodies.

So, the primary goal of energy workers is to help restore the system to its innate state of harmony. However, we may also treat the respective body system if we are guided to do so.

Energy work is largely guided by intuition. So, if we receive specific guidance to treat the system where a disease originated, we certainly do that in addition to treating the system as a whole.

Question 44

Why does the client's pain increase after a Reiki session and what to do about it?

A client of mine fell a few months ago and hit the right side of her head pretty badly. She's had MRI's, scans, and tests, and they reveal no physical damage. However, she suffers from constant pain on the right side of her head, she said it feels like a stabbing pain right above her ear.

This is her second session of Reiki with me. I asked her to rate the pain before I started working on her, and she said it was about a 5.

After our session I asked her to rate the pain, and she actually said that while I was working on her, the pain subsided quite a bit, almost to the point of it going away, but never went away completely as I worked on her.

After our session she said the pain actually felt like it was more of a 6. So the pain increased a bit.

Can you tell me what might cause this?

Deb's answer:

I believe your client's situation is not an uncommon one we experience in doing Reiki work.

Although all the medical tests have had negative results, this does not mean there are no physical reasons for this client's stabbing pains. Decades ago, when x-rays were first used, it seemed to be a medical miracle – and it was! Now we have CAT scans, MRI's, and other tests; and an x-ray can seem rudimentary. It is possible there is an injury, not yet detectable.

In the second session, when the client's pain almost subsided, and then went higher than the beginning point, this indicates the healing process is working. Reiki assists our bodies in repairing injuries, more quickly and more efficiently. This may entail some discomfort, or pain – not unlike a broken bone repairing itself – except with Reiki, the healing process can become condensed in a shorter period of time. It can be more intense.

For future sessions with this client, it may be helpful to focus equally on all her chakras, setting the intention for whole mind, body, spirit healing. This fall had to be traumatic for her and could affect her entire system. Balancing all her energetic centers will be helpful. Additionally, there may be a message, or a life lesson for her to grasp, and another chakra may hold the root cause of the issue. For example, falls can indicate an imbalance in life, or rushing too much, or not taking sufficient care of our bodies. Giving Reiki to all the chakras may be important.

It is obvious you approach each session with good intentions and a loving spirit. Simply continue to do that, and know that Reiki will always bring healing, in whatever form your client needs. Many blessings!

Question 45

Why does Reiki feel warm some times, and cold other times?

When I do Reiki my hands are hot, and the patient or client feels the heat. But sometimes my hands are ice cold and this reflects on the person too. Could you explain the cold energy please? Thank you.

Angie's answer:

It is not uncommon for Reiki practitioners and their clients to feel a number of sensations during a Reiki session. Heat is the one we hear about the most, but people often feel other sensations, such as tingling or pulsing or cold or momentary pain or discomfort as they are giving or receiving Reiki. These are all ways that we sense energy blockages moving, shifting and releasing within the client as the Reiki energy moves through them.

When you feel cold, instead of heat, it is because the type or density of the energy that needs to be cleared is different from in another situation where you have felt heat.

In a situation where you are feeling a stronger sensation of any type, no matter if it's cold, heat, tingling or whatever, that is a signal to stay in that area and send Reiki until the sensation eases away. Reiki is working to clear energy there and the energy is responding. In other words, the cold you feel should be seen as a good sign that the Reiki is working exactly as it needs to, just as it always does!

Deb's answer:

During Reiki sessions, I have intuitively received these messages about the sensations in my hands as well.

A few times when I experienced coldness, what I intuited was that a specific chakra area was depleted of energy as the client had overexpended energy, without replenishing it. I remember one client who worked as a nurse and gave much compassion to each patient she was assigned, and her heart chakra felt "empty." During our discussion after the session, she started to talk about the emptiness she feels within her personal life. She noted she is in a difficult marriage and does not feel loved and supported by her husband. So, she gave love, but was receiving little love back into her heart.

Other times, what I have been told about sensations in my hands is that they correspond to the type of energy that is being channeled into the client. For example, some clients need powerful energies, corresponding to the solar plexus chakra. For me, it feels like an electrical power surge went through my body, and my hands feel huge. Or, other clients may need nurturing and compassion, and I feel the gentleness flowing through my hands. Yet others may need security and solid grounding energies and the energies feel secure and confident. As each of us practices Reiki more and more, these nuances may become more evident.

However, it is not necessary to identify and understand what is happening energetically for the client. We only need to trust that Reiki always works for the client's highest good, and healing will occur where needed, and at the right time.

Question 46

Why am I getting pain in a certain area while doing Reiki for a client?

At times I feel pain while doing Reiki on someone. Am I getting the pain in a certain area because the client has that problem?

Ashwita's answer:

If you are feeling pain merely while healing and it doesn't stay on after the healing is over, then there is nothing to worry about and yes, you are most likely taking on a little bit of pain from the client as it passes through you. It is more like a reflection than an absorption, and while most of the times you will find that the client has a physical problem in the area where you are experiencing the pain, on some rare occasions you will find that the pain you are experiencing might be a physical manifestation of the emotional state of your client – for example, a pain in the throat might indicate the person has trouble expressing their feelings.

If the pain persists after the healing, then it means you are picking up the client's energies, and it is important to ensure that you wash your hands and feet after the healing, or even take a shower if the healing was too intense. You could also use sea salt to cleanse yourself at the end of healing.

Question 47

What are the meanings of sensations I feel when giving a Reiki treatment?

When giving a Reiki treatment, what are the meanings of sensations I feel? For instance, does heat or tingling mean that there is lots of energy being used and that the area needs a longer treatment? Is it different for every practitioner and we just use our intuition as to why we're feeling a particular thing?

Haripriya's answer:

Generally speaking, all sensations- heat, cold and tingling- indicate that energy is flowing to a specific area. Most people perceive this flow as heat and tingling, while some perceive it as cold. Some practitioners also report sensations of cold in areas that hold major blockages. However, there are no stringent pointers, as energy flow is perceived differently by different people. It is more important to trust our intuition as to what a certain sensation means in a specific healing scenario.

Heat and tingling often indicate that an area needs more healing. However, this is not true all of the time. The best course of action is to follow your hands. Allow your hands to rest on different chakras for as long as they feel like. When an area is sufficiently healed, your hands will automatically shift to the next position. Regular practice is the most effective way to understand the subtle working of energy.

Patti's answer:

Common sensations felt by the healer in a Reiki session include heat, coldness, and tingling. These are typically felt in the hands, but you also may also get sensations "mirrored" in your own body, corresponding to the area of discomfort. Reiki energy will always flow to where it is needed, however if you feel drawn to a specific area, by all means, give it extra attention. Length of treatment is usually determined in advance. Depending on what you experience during the session, a second treatment may be recommended, however I would not extend the initial agreed upon session duration.

Sensations do vary by practitioner. You may become aware of resistance or you may sense a certain color or pattern. Pay attention and let your intuition guide you. Remember that we are the conduit of the energy and are not required to, nor should we, attempt to diagnose or give medical advice. Call on your spirit guides for assistance and trust that the recipient will get exactly the healing they need.

Question 48

What can I do to increase my sensitivity to Reiki?

Sometimes I don't feel anything at all when giving Reiki treatments. This makes me doubt if Reiki is indeed flowing through me and if the treatments I give would be effective or not. What can I do to increase my sensitivity to Reiki?

Angie's answer:

This is a very common question among Reiki practitioners. It is not uncommon at all to have sessions in which you feel little or nothing. It is almost never anything to concern yourself with. Reiki will flow if it is your intention for it to flow and your client's intention to receive. Here are some tips to help you feel more connected and relaxed:

1. I encourage you not to worry about the Reiki flow and to practice the principle, "Just for today, I will not worry." Worry can actually feel very much like it is blocking or restricting the flow of Reiki because it is restricting your own personal energy flow.
2. Make sure you are doing daily self-Reiki practice, even if only for a few minutes.
3. Always give yourself Reiki for a few minutes prior to a Reiki session. Also send Reiki to the walls and the Reiki table. This will establish the connection and ease any nerves or worries you may have. Even if you don't notice any change right away, you will notice a difference between a session where you did this and one where you did not.
4. Make a point of intending to connect with Reiki many times throughout the day so that you become more familiar with the different ways it can feel. It is often very subtle, yet you can see the effect it has, so you know it is working.
5. Check in with your client after the session to see what their experience was. You might be very surprised to see that they felt many things, even though you felt little or

nothing. Check in with them again several days later to see how they are feeling. These are good practices for you to understand how the energy is working and to help you evaluate the progress of treatment.

Ashwita's answer:

How one responds to Reiki is a very personal thing, and this changes from time to time. Someone who is very sensitive in the beginning can find themselves feeling nothing at all for months, and someone who felt nothing at all for the first few months might become extremely sensitive over a period of time. In some cases, people might feel nothing at all even after years of healing and this is perfectly fine.

It is important to understand that feelings have nothing to do with the intensity or effectiveness of healing. A sensitive person who is not yet ready for deep healing might feel a lot of things but really not experience much of a difference in life – or not really facilitate a deep healing. On the other hand, a not so sensitive person who is truly ready for a big leap spiritually or with respect to healing, might feel nothing at all but find their lives changing radically after the Reiki healing – or bring about a deep shift in a client. If you want to be an effective Reiki healer, avoid comparing your experiences with others because each person is different. Instead, focus on strengthening your Reiki practice and make sure you're very regular.

It is of course; understandable that one might feel unconfident while healing others if there are no feelings. To address this issue, try healing more people. Once you start receiving feedback of how they are feeling better even when you felt nothing, you will start to develop confidence.

Personally, I believe that a lack of sensitivity more often than not, allows a person to facilitate deeper healing because the mind cannot interfere with the healing at all. When there are feelings, the mind tends to interfere and try to come up with solutions for the problems it perceives, instead of letting Reiki do the work. Among my students who facilitate the deepest healing, many feel nothing at all.

Question 49

What can I do to be able to do Byosen Scan?

I have never been able to Byosen Scan, nor sense the energy of the recipient, and only recently have I been able to sense the Reiki flow from my hands, and only if I rub them together before giving Reiki. I have been attuned to 2nd degree since 2002. Why is that, and what can I do about it?

Patti's answer:

In using the Byosen technique in Reiki, we are scanning the body with our hand(s) to look for imbalance or sickness in the body. Common sensations felt in the hands while scanning are warmth, coldness, and/or tingling. Each may indicate something different, however as a Reiki healer, it is not necessary to attempt a diagnosis. We simply give these areas extra attention during the healing session.

To scan, hold your hand two or three inches above the body and slowly move down toward the feet. Some healers prefer the left hand, some the right. I sometimes use both hands depending on where I am scanning on the body. There really is no prescribed method that must be followed. This is an intuitive practice, so use what works for you. Remember, in Reiki you are never alone. Call on your spirit guides for assistance and follow your intuition.

As your hand moves, note any changes in temperature or any sensations of tingling, pain, or discomfort you might feel in your palm. These are often very subtle so don't get discouraged if you don't feel much of anything. A normal healthy body may not have any obvious signs of imbalance. If you don't feel sensations, simply continue the treatment as usual. On occasion, you may feel sensation in your own body corresponding with where you are scanning on the client. This is just another way energy blocks can be discovered.

In answer to your second question, connection to energy is achieved through breath and intent. You are attuned to Reiki II and that's great. You should already have a strong connection that is maintained by regular practice. To improve your energy flow and sensation, try scheduling an energy session for yourself. Over time, the stress of daily life creates imbalance in our emotions and our bodies. You may have blocks that need clearing. A good massage by a Reiki attuned therapist will work wonders for clearing stuck energy. If you are still feeling a lack of energy flow, add daily meditation to increase your connection to spirit and to nature.

Question 50

How can one learn to scan aura?

How can one who cannot see auras learn to scan auras? And where to start?

Patti's answer:

We all have different gifts that we can use in our healing practices. If your ability to see auras is not as strong as some, you may have another talent that is equally as useful. Explore your gifts and use the ones that work best for you.

That being said, learning to see auras is something that can improve with practice. It may or may not be something you feel you need to strengthen once you explore other areas that may come more naturally to you.

Try this exercise when in a crowded place such a meeting, a classroom, on public transportation, etc. Sit or stand toward the back so you can see most of the room. Quietly take some deep breaths to relax, center yourself, and connect to energy. Allow your eyes to soften and become unfocused, then let your gaze move slowly around the room. You should be able to see a hazy outline, 2 or 3 inches wide, around some of the people. Auras are not the same for everyone. They vary according to mood, physical health and general wellbeing. A vibrant person may have a strong, visible aura, while a low energy or depressed person's may be barely visible.

Auras can have color to them, but not always and not to every healer. Look for breaks or difference in consistency, as well as the strength of the aura itself. You can also look at your own aura in a mirror. Do this in a moderately lit room, as opposed to a very bright one. Stand in front of the mirror. Look at your reflection. Then look away or close your eyes and center yourself. Use your strong breath to connect to energy, then check your reflection again. Does it look different? Do you see an outline around your profile? What I see when I do this is a

2 to 3-inch halo of energy around myself. You may see something different. Whatever you see, trust it and continue to explore. Practice makes perfect.

Question 51

Should the healer continue giving Reiki or stop when the client experiences a healing crisis?

While giving Reiki to a client, many times the client experiences a healing crisis. In that scenario, should the healer continue giving Reiki or stop?

Deb's answer:

Healing crises come in many forms – a client may shed tears, become nauseous, feel agitated or distressed, or display other symptoms of discomfort. If it seems the client needs to take a little break from receiving Reiki, the practitioner may offer to stop giving Reiki for a few minutes. The practitioner should offer a tissue, a drink of water, or another appropriate aid. More importantly, the practitioner needs to take the opportunity to provide reassurance to the client. This comforting support includes giving the client education about a healing crisis – simply that an issue, or blockage, has arisen to be healed. It is a positive step in the healing process as the person is now ready to deal with this issue, and release its negative impact. If the client wants to talk about the experience, the practitioner becomes an active listener by giving full attention to the client's words and not giving advice. If the client does not say anything, accept this choice, as he may need more time to reflect on what occurred.

After a brief break, the practitioner should continue to give Reiki for the remaining time. This will assist the client to continue his healing process. It also reinforces the belief Reiki never causes harm and always creates healing. All of us know that healing is not a smooth, straightforward road. We will have challenging times as we walk the healing path. Remember that Reiki brings loving and healing energies, and it is always directed to the client's highest good.

Question 52

Is it possible to give Reiki to a group of people all at once? How would one go about that?

Patti's answer:

While it is possible to send Reiki to a group, the students might have a more powerful experience if they were allowed to explore their own energy. Start with an overview of what Reiki is and move on to a simple guided meditation. For a classroom setting where the students are seated in chairs, ask them to sit up tall with their feet firmly planted on the floor, grounding to earth. In a more informal setting, they can sit cross legged on the floor with the root of the spine firmly connected to earth. Start them off with some deep breaths to relax, then ask them to close their eyes and envision a white ball of energy moving through their body, starting with the feet and moving slowly up until it reaches the crown. Finish the mediation with three more deep breaths, and have them open their eyes. You can then have a group discussion. Ask for volunteers to share how it felt to each of them individually.

Deb's answer:

It is simple to send Reiki to multiple recipients at one time. Use the distance-healing symbol, and set the intention for the Reiki energies to go to each person. With Universal Life Force Energy, everything is possible and there are no limitations. It is also possible to send Reiki to a situation where many people are involved; this may be to a workplace issue, a natural disaster, a family crisis, or any situation with a few, dozens or thousands, of people involved.

This answer is with the assumption that recipients have not paid the practitioner a fee for a distance healing session. If Reiki is a paid service, the client is entitled to receive individual Reiki for the amount of time paid. One reason for this is the Reiki practitioner focuses on one person only, sending Reiki specifically for the highest good of the client. It is possible the practitioner may receive energetic impressions for the client. This guideline maintains integrity for the client, and for Reiki practice.

Question 53

How to approach Reiki on someone who says they are ready to receive Reiki but energetically they are not?

What is the best way to approach Reiki on someone who says they are ready to receive, yet, energetically, has thick walls and clearly does not want to receive?

Angie's answer:

Prior to starting a session, especially with a new client, always let them know that if they become uncomfortable with a hand position or with the treatment itself, to let you know so you can stop. Make sure they know that you will not do anything they don't want you to do.

Sometimes a person can ask for Reiki and yet they are still very nervous about receiving it. They may be unsure what to expect, have issues with being vulnerable, or other issues that cause them to have trouble relaxing. If they have asked for Reiki, I would trust that they are indeed willing to receive it and are ready to begin working with the blocks that are holding them back. The blocks will begin to be dissolved, at a rate that they are able to tolerate, by the Reiki treatments. Many times, someone who has a great deal of blocked energy will also have a lot of cords. If you detect cords, it may be a good thing to ask if they would like you to do a cord cutting (if you have been trained in that). If they agree, then proceed.

A person who feels stiff and blocked needs you to be relaxed and confident even more than most people, so try to stay relaxed. Ask Reiki to flow to any concerns or fears you may have about the situation. If you ever feel that a person has changed their mind about receiving Reiki, simply stop and check in with them about their comfort level.

Question 54

Is it all right to send Reiki to someone without their permission?

Deb's answer:

This is a thought-provoking question, and the fact that you are asking it demonstrates the value you place on Reiki. It is not unusual for any of us to pray for a person, without asking their permission. Sometimes, it is not possible to reach the person, or he would not be able to respond, due to being in a nonresponsive state or in another location. We pray because we believe in its power and know it is always good.

Reiki is the same – it is always good and never causes harm. We must be clear in the intention that it is for the highest good of the person, and we should not state what we think the highest good is! We cannot see the "big picture" and what we think is best for someone may not be the case. The Universe will send the healing as needed.

If this feels uncomfortable to you, there is another option. You can set the intention to send Reiki to the person. Ask your Higher Self to ask the other's Higher Self (or soul) if it will receive Reiki energies. You can state that if the Higher Self does not want Reiki, the energies will be sent to Mother Earth.

Question 55

Is it better for the client to be lying down or seated?

I have mostly given Reiki when the recipient is seated. Which do you think is better, lying down or seated?

Ashwita's answer:

Every healer works differently, and what works amazingly with one might not be so great with another. Having said that, I prefer my clients to be lying down unless intuitively guided otherwise, which does happen.

Lying down allows a person to relax more easily and more deeply, which might just help them integrate the healing better. Healing them while seated is a great option when the client is pregnant or having back trouble, as it gives us easy access to the back chakras.

If you heal your clients while they're seated because of intuitive guidance, then that is the best way you can facilitate healing. However, if you're in doubt, I would suggest healing some clients seated, and others lying down, and seeing if their feedback varies. That will give you a clear picture.

Question 56

I used to practice until I was diagnosed with fibromyalgia and lupus. Am I right to feel that I must clear myself so that I can begin practicing again?

I used to practice Reiki until I was diagnosed with fibromyalgia and lupus. Since my diagnosis I haven't been able to even perform my daily self-healing. I feel like a clogged pipe and no water can get through. Am I right to feel that I must clear myself so that I can begin practicing again? I have cleared my chakras but I feel that they become blocked again very quickly. I feel that I must have them all clear before I start to practice Reiki again. Am I right? Or, will I become unblocked if I just start back with my daily self-healing routine? I am a bit confused about how to get back to being able function as a Reiki practitioner.

Angie's answer:

Having Fibromyalgia myself, I can understand exactly what you are experiencing. During a flare-up, I feel that same clogged pipe feeling. It can feel very discouraging to do self-Reiki. However, I encourage you to continue doing daily self-treatment. It does make a difference. The more Reiki you have flowing into you, the faster you will feel better. Also send Reiki to your water, food and bath or shower water to boost your healing in every possible way. If you are taking medications or supplements, send Reiki to them as well. I also encourage you to seek treatment from another practitioner during flare-ups. That can help to clear them much more quickly and give you the opening to clear that clogged pipe feeling.

If you don't feel comfortable practicing on other people while you feel blocked and ill, then follow your own guidance about that. Your own intuition knows what you need to do and will know when you are ready to return to treating others again.

Chapter 10 – Protection

Question 57

How do you know if you're using your own energy during healing?

Haripriya's answer:

When practitioners use their personal reserve of energy for healing, they normally begin to feel drained and exhausted.

In contrast, when we act as channels for Universal energies such as Reiki to flow through us, we do not feel drained. We feel light and joyful. The process of offering healing feels effortless. We also feel refreshed as the energy courses through us and flows to the recipient. Many Reiki practitioners report that they also feel like recipients of a Reiki treatment while they offer Reiki to others.

The bottom-line is that using our limited energy feels constricting while opening up to higher energies feels nourishing.

Question 58

Can the practitioner absorb negative energy from the client?

When giving a Reiki session to a client, can the practitioner unintentionally absorb negative energies from the client? I learned techniques to use the symbols for protection on myself and in the room before starting a Reiki session, but I also heard from someone who is very intuitive and can "see" energies that some of the "bad" energies can stay in the practitioner.
What are the odds that the energies will be absorbed?

Ashwita's answer:

There is a difference between a 'healer' and a 'channel'. As a Reiki channel, all you do is facilitate the flow of Reiki and it is Reiki that makes the healing happen. In this case you pick up nothing, and the energies in almost all cases do not even pollute the space in which the healing is done.

However, we are human beings and we make mistakes. When we get involved with the client either consciously or subconsciously, then some energies remain behind after healing. In most cases if this energy residue is minimal, there is almost no instantaneous effect, but a cumulative one in the long run if the self-healing practice is not strong enough.

Contrary to popular perception, protection can often create a more dangerous environment, because in most cases it is motivated by fear. Fear is heavy energy and creates blocks, which create spaces where any stray negative energies from the client can get stuck in your system. I say that protection is 'often' dangerous because this isn't always the case. I have seen people who use it simply for the sake of convenience do just fine. Most sensitive people I know need to replace protection with Reiki flooding for better results though.

I teach my students to ask themselves one critical question before they heal anyone – 'is this person's pain causing me pain?' If the answer is yes even remotely, it is better to start the healing by healing one's own feelings first, and then moving on to the client after one is comfortable.

Question 59

Do healers get the clients' disease, or are interfering with that person's karma?

Many people are afraid to heal others as they believe that they might get the person's disease or they are interfering with that person's karma. How far is it true?

Haripriya's answer:

If this were true, the medical community would be the most seriously afflicted. They would take on the karma of all the patients they treat round the clock. This is obviously not the case because medical personnel only do their job of providing supportive care to someone who needs it or asks for it.

It is the same with energy healers too. We only act as channels for healing energy to flow through and to reach a recipient in the way that he or she needs it. How one receives the energy and the extent of healing are determined by the recipient's higher choices. We can never force a healing on someone who does not wish to heal.

The only time someone may initiate a karmic cycle would be if he or she makes false promises of healing or tries to force a healing upon someone who does not wish to heal. As practitioners, all we need to do is stick to our job of channeling energy for the greater good of the recipient and not get attached to the outcome.

Question 60

How do I protect myself from picking up client's energy?

How do I give Reiki through myself, rather than of myself, and how do I protect myself from picking up the clients' bad karma or bad attachments? How do I come through a session better off than I started without releasing my own goodness into the client? I need to release God's goodness into the client, have it come through me, not of me.

Ashwita's answer:

This is a really wonderful question. It is a problem many people have faced, especially empaths.

I recommend asking yourself one question before you begin healing: Does this person's situation bring me pain? You know, like when you see someone suffering, and you really want them to get better soon. That is when you will end up giving them your own energies.

If you feel bad when you see this person suffering, or sometimes it could even be fear over *will I pick up her symptoms too?* – in either case, just feel your own pain or fear and request Reiki to resolve it. When you start developing a deep faith that every bit of suffering in anyone's life is a part of your own spiritual journey, you stop picking up their pain. When this knowledge isn't there, you want to remove your suffering and end up manipulating your energies subconsciously. This is when you take up their pain.

You are here as a part of this person's journey, placed here by life, by Reiki. All you need to do is step back and allow Reiki to do whatever is best for this person. Don't be attached to the results, and you'll do just fine.

One additional thing I like to do is to request Reiki to heal me as well as the client when I'm healing. In that way, anything I might have picked up by mistake is also healed.

Patti's answer:

In regards to your question how can a Reiki session be through myself and not of myself – in your question I hear that you may be concerned about giving too much of yourself in a session, giving away your power or picking up something from the client, such as an attachment, negative energy, or bad karma.

When we call in Reiki energy, we become the vessel through which the energy travels. With breath and intention, we call in Universal Healing Energy and that energy flows through us to the client. It's not our personal energy and once it is flowing, it does not require any effort on our part. Giving a treatment does not deplete us in any way. We become like a hollow reed.

That being said, there are things we can do in regards to self-protection. Many of us are empathic and sensitive to the moods and emotions of others. Clients may have negative attachments and we want to be sure we have done some preparation prior to the session.

First, create a sacred space. Prior to the session, call in Reiki energy and use the symbols available to you to cleanse the space. Repeat until you've done this in all four directions of the room. When I do a Reiki session, I call in my spirit guides, my angels, and my ancestors. In that way, I am never alone and not using my own power. You can call in an angel and ask for protection. I call in Archangel Michael and I ask that he shield me in a pure white protective light. You can call any angel or helping spirit you feel a connection with.

Be sure that you are properly grounded and feel your feet connect deeply with Mother Earth. You may also carry a protective crystal such as black tourmaline, smoky quartz, or another stone that resonates with you.

Elements can be used to transmute negative energy. Simply allowing water to run over your hands after a session will remove anything you may have picked up. Or you can imagine a pure violet flame cleansing your aura.

Do these things and proceed with your session with confidence that you are loved and protected.

Question 61

What is the best shielding and best grounding mechanism when giving a client Reiki?

I am an intuitive empath that does Reiki. No matter the shielding mechanism I use I absorb the clients' issues like a sponge. What is the best shielding and grounding mechanism when giving a client Reiki?

Ashwita's answer:

Shielding and protection rarely work for sensitive people as the basis of protection is fear and separation and they do not reflect the deeper spiritual truth – that we are all one.

The best way to protect oneself not only during healing but also when with people we perceive as negative, is to flood yourself and others with Reiki energy.

To do this, imagine that energy is pouring in through the top of your head and filling up every cell in your body, and your body is now overflowing with energy and flooding the client / person so that their whole system is cleansed and full of light. You can also flood your room or house during this process to clear out any residual energies.

Read more about flooding:
http://reikirays.com/16561/energy-flooding-with-reiki/

Question 62

Is it possible to repel an energy vampire using Reiki?

Ashwita's answer:

The easiest way is to simply avoid interacting with such people, but in the event that that is not possible, there are ways to protect oneself.

Energy vampires take energy from us by presenting us with opportunity after opportunity to sympathize, which causes us to give them our energy. After we have identified them as energy vampires, it is much easier, because now just our fear of them will dislodge energy from our system and flow towards them.

So if you want to protect yourself from energy vampires due to fear, then no matter what method you try, it will not work. Fear has only one antidote, love. For this reason, I find the term energy vampire disturbing because it puts a very disturbing label on another human being, one that evokes fear – it is very hard to love an energy vampire as one of 'us', right?

When you are in the presence of the 'energy vampire', stay grounded in love. Watch any fear that tries to crop up inside you, and let it be – don't touch it. If you love yourself, you will not encourage any fearful thoughts. When you look at this person, look at them with compassion, seeing through their behavior into a person who is just identified with their pain.

You cannot be left devoid of energy if there is a continuous flow. So simply being in acceptance of the situation (ok, I HAVE to spend an hour with this person) and practicing Reiki (you can keep it flowing continuous by Reiki-ing your knees or thighs) is enough. You could even practice Reiki flooding.

Chapter 11 – Business and Marketing

Question 63

How do you find the first paying clients?

How do people find their first paying clients? How do they find their first students when they are at the Master level and ready to teach?

Patti's answer:

To find paying clients and students to teach, a Reiki practitioner must be visible to the public. There are many ways to do this and there are entire courses on how to start a Reiki business. Following are a few suggestions. For more information, I would encourage you to look into a professional course.

Find a space to hold a regular Reiki Share, free of charge or for an optional "love" donation. Do this one or twice a month. Depending on your location, you will most likely get a mixture of people; those who are curious about Reiki, and those who have tried Reiki and are looking for a place to practice. These are potential clients who may want to schedule future one-on-one sessions with you or take a class to increase their knowledge.

Offer classes – during your Reiki share, make sure there is information visible on session rates and upcoming classes. Use a sign in sheet to collect emails to send notice of future events.

Consider creating a website to list your services. Explore using social media to stir interest.

Create a handout with services offered and pricing. Tack this up on public bulletin boards that serve groups that are health conscious. Good places to start are yoga studios or natural food stores.

Volunteer at local hospitals to meet people and share Reiki face to face.

Once you have a client, make suggestions for future treatment and offer to book a return appointment.

Question 64

How does one differentiate themselves from other practitioners?

In an already saturated market, how does one differentiate oneself from other Reiki practitioners?

Deb's answer:

It can feel difficult to develop a successful Reiki practice in areas where they are several other practitioners. However, there are many positive realities in this situation. The first fact is that you live in an area where people are open-minded and accepting of Reiki as a complementary healing modality. Also, Reiki is known and you will not have to do a great amount of education required in areas where Reiki is still an unknown word and concept. You can build on existing knowledge in the community.

There are a number of ways to differentiate yourself from other practitioners. Identify your interests and your strengths. If you love animals, consider offering animal Reiki. If you are a comfortable presenter, give free Reiki information presentations at your local library or bookstore. If you are not a Reiki Master already, prayerfully consider if teaching Reiki is part of your life purpose. Not only will you demonstrate your commitment to Reiki as a way of life, you will also be able to offer Reiki trainings. When there is a choice of several practitioners, many clients will choose the one who has the highest level of training. Another possibility is to be trained in other healing modalities, such as massage therapy, sacral cranial work, aromatherapy, color therapy, or acupressure. Some Reiki practitioners have had much success with offering Reiki circles, having a booth at a local festival, writing articles for local publications, and utilizing other ways of becoming known in their community.

And, most important of all, continue to practice self-treatments of Reiki frequently. When a Reiki practitioner works on keeping his own energy at a high, positive level, he attracts clients to his practice. He grows in gratitude and peacefulness – potential clients will feel this energy and schedule a Reiki session with you.

Question 65

How do I get my Reiki clients to come back for regular treatment?

Deb's answer:

The most important task for a Reiki practitioner is to be an open, loving instrument for the possibility of healing for a client. The experience begins with a welcoming and pleasant atmosphere. The treatment room is aesthetically pleasing, and the practitioner is genuine and compassionate. The intention of the practitioner is always for the highest good of the client.

One factor to recognize and accept is that clients always have a choice whether or not to schedule more sessions. Perhaps, there are financial or time constraints. Or, during a session, an issue arises for healing, but the client chooses not to deal with the issue yet and avoids another session. Sometimes, a client receives guidance to pursue another alternative modality, such as massage therapy or acupuncture.

When a client is deeply touched by Reiki, it is common for her to find a Reiki class and become attuned herself. She has a strong desire to give Reiki to family and friends, practice self-treatment and maybe start her own practice. This decision is a very positive outcome in Reiki practice, although there may not be a direct financial benefit for the first practitioner.

Every person is on a journey to healing and wholeness. Whenever a Reiki practitioner contributes to another's journey, a successful practice exists. Positive word-of-mouth will happen, and new clients will want to schedule Reiki sessions with you.

Question 66

What is the best way to ensure your safety?

What is the best way to ensure your safety when working with clients, assuming the two of you are alone?

Deb's answer:

The fact that you are asking this question is the first step in assuring safety – awareness is the most important element. When working with the public, one should always be aware of the environment and think of ways to make it safer. The first consideration is thoughtfully setting up your treatment room to enhance safety. This may include factors such as a clear path to exit quickly if needed; being aware of other practitioners in your building; a good hiding place for handbags, wallets, etc. You should have easy access to your cellphone at all times.

One of the most important aspects of awareness is recognizing "red flags." A red flag is a small incident that simply does not feel right. For example, a client makes a few odd comments. Or, the client makes a mildly suggestive statement, or touches you in a "too friendly" way. You have a gut feeling something is "off"; listen to your gut! Address the uncomfortable comments or touches immediately, setting a boundary that this behavior is unacceptable in a treatment situation. (Not saying anything is akin to giving permission for the client to continue.) If the client does not stop the behavior, end the session and ask him or her to leave.

There are certain situations where you need to end the session and ask the client to leave immediately. Some examples of these are: the client is clearly inebriated or affected by drug use; the client threatens violence; the client makes strong sexual statements. If the client does not leave, you must leave the room – and make sure you take your cellphone with you. Depending on the circumstances, you may need to call the local police. Most important of all – do whatever is necessary to keep yourself safe.

Chapter 12 – Reiki as Complementary Therapy

Question 67

Is Reiki effective against chronic conditions (Cancer, MS, Diabetes, etc.)?

Angie's answer:

Reiki has not been extensively studied for its effectiveness in treatment of these types of illness in scientific research. However, it has been shown to be helpful for a great number of people with chronic conditions such as cancer and MS in relieving the pain, discomfort and symptoms associated with the illness in many studies. It has been shown to be so helpful in reducing the pain associated with cancer and the anxiety that often accompanies treatment that many prominent hospitals in the United States, such as the Mayo Clinic and the Cleveland Clinic, are now offering it to their patients.

There are quite a few cases in which patients who had a chronic illness report recovering after receiving regular Reiki treatments and/or receiving level one training and beginning to self-treat. These were typically cases in which the patient was actively involved in their own wellness in many ways – body, mind and spirit. They also continued to follow up with their medical doctor until they were well. Reiki may have played a role in helping them to recover and they certainly seem to think so, though the medical community is not so sure.

Question 68

Is it advisable to do Reiki on someone with cancer?

Is it advisable to do Reiki on someone with cancer? I have had a Master tell me that it isn't done, because it feeds energy to the cancer cells. My counter argument is that Reiki can do no harm. Can Reiki harm cancer patients?

Deb's answer:

You are correct in thinking that Reiki will do no harm. The source of Reiki is divine Universal Life Force Energy. This spiritual wisdom always knows exactly which areas a person would most benefit from healing within the physical, emotional / mental and spiritual aspects. When a person has cancer, the healing energies may be directed many ways. In the physical realms, the energies may strengthen the healthy cells while decreasing, or possibly eliminating, the cancer cells. The energies may also decrease pain or inflammation; or, enhance the positive effects of medical treatments such as chemotherapy or radiation.

Perhaps the Reiki Master who gave you this information was influenced by beliefs massage therapists and other practitioners have regarding clients with cancer. There is some concern that physical manipulation of malignant tumors can cause growth and spread of cancer cells. Reiki, however, does not include this kind of work. The Reiki practitioner gently places her hands upon the client, or can keep her hands a few inches above the skin's surface. Either way, no harm will come to the client.

Question 69

How to give Reiki for Parkinson's disease patients?

How to give Reiki for Parkinson's disease? What are the steps involved, and can it be cured?

Angie's answer:

Reiki does not promise a cure of any illness. It would be inappropriate for any treatment to promise a cure for something, as this can't be guaranteed. However, Reiki can help to bring balance to the underlying issues and it can also help to ease the symptoms and the distress they bring. I don't know of any scientific studies that have been done with Reiki and Parkinson's patients, but I have read personal stories of patients who have been helped by it.

Treating a Parkinson's patient with Reiki is much the same as treating any other patient. Make any adjustments you may need to for their comfort and wellbeing during the treatment. For example, you may need to treat them from a chair, rather than asking them to get up on a treatment table, if their disease has progressed to a point where that would be challenging for them.

Sometimes patients with neurological conditions have difficulty receiving treatment directly on the head at the beginning of the treatment and do better if you start in another area, such as the feet. Do a whole body treatment, just as you would with any other client. If it's possible, treat the spine as well, but if it isn't accessible, send distant Reiki to it or ask Reiki to flow there during treatment.

Deb's answer:

Parkinson's Disease results from a progressive brain disorder. Some of the symptoms include tremors, rigid muscles, slowed movement, loss of balance, and eventually changes in speech and writing abilities.

Since it affects the entire body, I would recommend doing the full, one-hour body treatment as frequently as possible. Spending additional time with your hands on the person's head may be helpful.

The promise of Reiki is that healing is always brought to the receiver. This healing may manifest itself by decreasing the symptoms. Physical conditions are not necessarily cured and leave the body completely through the use of Reiki – although miracles can always happen. With Parkinson's Disease, it is possible the tremors may become less severe, or balanced walking is improved. These improvements can certainly add to the quality of life, and will be greatly appreciated by the patient.

The intention the Reiki practitioner brings to the channeling of the Universal Life Force Energy is always for the highest good of the receiver. The Divine always responds with healing energies. Sometimes, the energies do result in some physical improvements. Also, the energies can help decrease distressing emotions, such as sadness or non-acceptance; or assist in spiritual growth for the receiver. Healing occurs in many forms.

Please continue with frequent Reiki treatments, trusting that the loving, healing energies will make a difference. Trust that the results are exactly what this person needs in his, or her, life journey. Many blessings!

Question 70

How does Reiki help in treating autism?

How does Reiki help in treating autism? What chakras and points should be covered for giving Reiki to Autistic children?

Angie's answer:

While there is currently no known cure for autism, Reiki can be a great tool in the treatment of autism. Reiki is a therapy that helps to bring balance and ease to the person receiving it, regardless of their condition.

Some of the ways that Reiki can benefit someone with autism are: easing anxiety and bringing greater calm, helping to bring better sleep quality, soothing the nervous system, soothing the digestive system, bringing greater overall relaxation to both the mind and the body, and easing tight muscles.

One of the great things about using Reiki as a tool in the treatment of autism is that it can be used either hands on or with the hands slightly above the body. Some people may even prefer to receive Reiki from across the room or even at a greater distance and with Reiki, you always have that flexibility.

You can also modify the treatment each time as needed. For example, you may need to start at the feet instead of the head, or some other position, or do whatever is most appropriate for the child in that instance.

Pay attention to what seems to be right for them and follow their lead each time as this will make each Reiki session the most beneficial for them.

Regular Reiki treatments will be the most beneficial, so either having a regular Reiki therapist or a parent in the house who is attuned can be very useful.

Reiki can be a great tool to help cope with some of that challenges that can arise with autism, bringing greater balance and easing distress, soothing and relieving physical aliments. The child and the parent may both decide to become attuned to the first level of Reiki themselves at some point, so that they can always have this tool available, without having to wait for an appointment when an immediate need arises.

Patti's answer:

A Reiki session for an autistic child should follow the same general guidelines you would typically use in your practice on adults, children and animals. Worry less about hitting all the chakra points and more about the comfort of the recipient. Keep in mind that the reactions of those receiving Reiki will differ. Some will intuitively welcome the energy, others may need a more hands off approach and may even do better receiving Reiki from a few feet away. The age of the recipient will influence the experience as well. Be observant and go slowly. Work as lightly or deeply as your client's comfort level allows.

Remember that Reiki is intelligent energy and it will go to the areas that best serve your client. You are doing much good and will be providing benefits that can include better sleep, anxiety relief, increased concentration, **the ability to self-calm, as well as improved physical health and relief from discomfort.**

Question 71

Can Reiki help when dealing with severe depression?

Angie's answer:

Reiki is only recently beginning to be studied in depth by the scientific community to evaluate its medical benefits on individual conditions. While there is some research available about Reiki and depression, it is difficult to make a firm conclusion based on what little there is. There have been some studies on Reiki and depression in which all the participants improved with Reiki, whether done distantly or hands-on. Others were inconclusive or showed little or no improvement.

There are many people who have received Reiki regularly in addition to their depression treatment and report benefiting. The key seems to be regular treatment, especially in the beginning. It is also very important that you maintain good contact and a good rapport with your doctor and your counselor to help you with any adjustments that may need to be made in your care while receiving Reiki. Your medication dosages and other care may need to be adjusted, lowered or changed if you begin to improve. It is always wise and helpful to inform your doctor and other health professionals when you begin a new form of treatment, for this reason.

You may want to consider taking the first level of Reiki training in order to further help yourself by giving yourself daily self-Reiki, if you find that having regular Reiki is helpful for you. Having this tool available can help to bring greater balance and to maintain that in the days and years to come, through continued self-practice.

Question 72

Do antidepressants hinder the Reiki connection?

How do you feel about antidepressants and Reiki? Do you think it hinders the connection?

Deb's answer:

Medications do not hinder the connection between Reiki energies that originate from Universal Life Force Energy, and the Reiki receiver. Rather, Reiki can increase the effectiveness of medications shortening the length of time medications are indicated, or lowering the dosage needed.

Clinical depression is a serious disorder, affecting a person's body, mood and thoughts. For many decades, research studies have demonstrated that a combination of antidepressants and psychotherapy is the most effective modality in the treatment of clinical depression. In recent years, new research is demonstrating that adding Reiki to these modalities produces a greater level of effectiveness in treating depression and other mental health diagnoses.

If the only effect Reiki had was reducing stress and promoting relaxation, it would still be helpful for people who are experiencing depression. However, receiving Reiki has many more benefits, as it positively affects the physical, mental / emotional and spiritual aspects of a person. Its powerful, and gentle, energies bring healing to the entire being of a person.

Question 73

Does Reiki help with menopause?

Does Reiki have any effect on women who are suffering from the menopause? Is it possible that it would help with the symptoms?

Angie's answer:

Since Reiki is a method of treatment that brings balance to the entire body, it is safe to say that it would also bring balance to the hormones and the emotions during menopause.

Reiki works to help the body return to its own natural state of balance, also called homeostasis, more easily and quickly. One of the things that happen as the body returns to this state is the hormones balance out, including the ones that can trigger anxiety and stressful energy. While some people feel hot during a Reiki treatment, it is not necessarily an increase in hot flashes, but simply the energy moving through the body.

Many women report feeling fewer menopausal symptoms after taking Reiki training at the first level and beginning a daily self-Reiki practice.

Question 74

Does Reiki help with arthritis?

Deb's answer:

Reiki can bring healing to all chronic conditions, including arthritis. However, it is important to understand the difference between a cure and healing. A cure means the physical condition is no longer present in the body. Reiki does not guarantee that every condition will be cured, although Reiki treatments do have miraculous results at times.

Healing refers to any aspect of a person's physical, mental/emotional and spiritual being. Many times, Reiki will lessen, or alleviate, the effects of a disease. In the case of arthritis, Reiki may lessen the achiness caused by the disease, or allow the person to move their stiff fingers with more ease. Reiki may help the person with arthritis to become less worried about the possible worsening of the disease, or accept their physical limitations with grace.

Many diseases such as arthritis can bring great spiritual growth to a person. They may grow in gratitude, by realizing the many blessings in their lives. Or, they may pray more frequently asking for physical relief, or spiritual direction in seeking medical treatment. On a deeper level, a person may start to explore the reasons "why" this is happening to him. Is there a life lesson to be learned? Does he need to deal with his own mortality and think about the possibility of life after death? Does he embrace the illness as part of his life purpose?

Let us always approach Reiki with the conviction that healing is always a possibility, but a physical cure may not be the type of healing most needed.

Chapter 13 – Relationships

Question 75

How do you use Reiki to manifest a life partner?

How do you use Reiki to manifest a life partner / soul mate? I am attuned at level 2 but after 5 years of Reiki he still hasn't shown up.

Haripriya's answer:

In order to manifest anything, we must vibrate at the same level as that of our desires. When we achieve this vibration, we magnetically and effortlessly draw our desires to us. Being attuned to Reiki is only the first step. Thereafter, we must also continue to consciously work on ourselves so we can reach our highest soul potential.

Trying too hard to manifest something can block it.
Believing that we are not worthy enough to have our desires fulfilled can also create blocks to manifestation.

Daily Reiki practice will help us become aware of the blocks that we may be placing on our path. Once we become aware, the next step is to work towards releasing those blocks. This can be achieved through Reiki, prayer, affirmations, working one on one with a therapist or a combination of techniques (whatever feels most comfortable).

Once this healing occurs, our vibration shifts and we prepare ourselves to receive the blessings that we wish to manifest. Finally, it is also important to let go of attachment to the outcome and allow our desires to manifest in perfect divine timing. All of this happens easily when we are regular with Reiki practice and allow Reiki to be our guide.

Question 76

Does Reiki work for broken relationships?

How does Reiki work for broken relationships or for relationships that face misunderstandings?

Ashwita's answer:

Every interaction is an exchange of energy. When we feel positive emotions towards a person, we send them positive energy, and when we feel negative emotions towards a person we offload our negative energy on them, whether we express our feelings or not. This obviously has a deep impact on our relationships.

Relationships become difficult when people want more than they are willing to give. By intensifying Reiki practicing during this time, one reduces the need for energy from others, and is able to give energy more freely – and this makes all the difference. Once one is able to give energy more freely, in the physical realm this manifests as being able to see more easily the other person's perspective, forgive trivial things, and express more kindly the things that need to be expressed.

As for broken relationships, energetically the connection between such people is usually tattered and damaged, so healing both the people along with the relationship will help heal the energy between them. Free-will still remains at play so if after healing, one of the people doesn't want to re-establish contact, then nothing can be done, but the animosity will not remain.

Question 77

How to use cord cutting and Reiki to disconnect from a relationship?

I would like to find out about cord cutting and how to have the courage to take steps for my freedom. I've been in a very miserable relationship for the last twelve years and my husband was an alcoholic, drug addict, womanizer, and a pathological liar. Twelve plus years of this and I don't need it. It's been two years since he's spoken to or seen my son. He is living with another woman now and I need to get out of it. I am not finding the energy or the mindset to take action, to basically go to a lawyer and file for a divorce. He is not giving me any kind of maintenance or anything. Thank you!

Angie's answer:

"Cords" refer to the bands of energy that form between us and another person that we are in communication with. When our hearts or brains send out an energy signal to another, that signal is called a cord. When we aren't emotionally involved with the person, the cord drops away after the communication is over. In our personal relationships, the cords remain and they become thicker and stronger as we bond with the other in various ways. This is also true when we argue and otherwise create negative energy with another.

Those communication bonds, or cords, remain as does the negative energy from the emotional pain, unless we are able to release them in a healthy manner. As these store in our systems, they can cause even more difficulties in the relationship and also cause us to continue repeating the same unhealthy relationship patterns, until they are resolved. It's a good idea to regularly remove cords in your system, just as it is to remove negative energy. Cord cutting won't remove healthy cords. It will only cut unhealthy relationship cords that you wish to end, when you are ready.

It's a good idea to have a cord cutting performed by another Reiki professional, if possible. We can become too involved in our own problems to fully see all of the blocks that we need help with and another professional can see these more clearly. If that's not possible, then you can use the release ceremony** I wrote about on Reiki Rays, asking Archangel Michael and Archangel Metatron to assist you in removing any cords and negative energy that you are ready to release. You may like to speak to the cord and to the Higher Self of the person the cord is attached to. Let them know you'll be dissolving the cord at your end and ask if they are willing to also dissolve the cord at their end. Thank the cord for the purposes it has served in the past and ask it to release, with the help of Reiki and Archangel Michael.

To boost your intentions to move forward, you can create a plan, writing down all the things you feel you need to do or have in place in your life in order to move forward and be free. Also write down what you would truly like your life to look like; not just the things you don't want, but all the joys in life that you do want. Be as detailed as you want about how you want life to feel. Hold this list between your hands and send Reiki to it. Do that every day until all the things are achieved. Choose to take the first small step on the list and offer yourself Reiki whenever you feel fear or a lack of strength to move ahead. Write this plan up before you perform the release ceremony and cord cutting, that way it will be in your mind as part of your intentions. It will give you strength to know that you are working toward moving forward.

** Release ceremony article:
http://reikirays.com/27189/release-ceremony/

Chapter 14 – Job / Career

Question 78

How can Reiki help when looking for a new job?

I'm desperately looking for a job change. What do I do in Reiki to achieve that?

Ashwita's answer:

Before we begin, I hope you are already practicing Reiki self-healing every day. If not, it is very important you spend at least 30 minutes every day healing all the chakras on your body, front as well as back.

Now, assuming that you already have a steady practice, the real problem that I see here is not so much that you are desperate for a job change, but that your current job situation is such, that you're seeking some sort of relief.

The important question in this context is why?

Every situation in life brings us valuable life lessons, and if you practice Reiki regularly and are still unable to find a better job, it is important to review your current situation and ask yourself what lessons this current situation might be bringing for you, and focus on learning those lessons.

Every morning, when you reach work, ask yourself: if you were at your new job, how would you feel this morning? Great, right? So, tell yourself that you aren't going to wait for a new job to feel great. You're going to feel great right now and start your day off on that note. The rest will take care of itself.

In case you find that you're not feeling that great, just tune into your body, see if there's any sensations, any heaviness or discomfort anywhere. Give Reiki to that part of your body and request Reiki to resolve your emotions.

Along with this, you could also spend some time creating an intention slip where you write something like: (*Your Name*) has a good job with pay at high industry standards, with a supportive boss and colleagues, with a work profile that challenges him and helps him grow personally as well as professionally.

If you have learned level two, you could draw the Reiki symbols on the backside of the paper and just give Reiki to this paper every day.

Ultimately it's important to remember to surrender to the plan that life has for you, and also to the results that Reiki brings when you start asking for help.

Angie's answer:

I would recommend that you first begin with Reiki self-treatment. This is always the very best place to start when we are facing a challenge in life because it helps to clear and heal any underlying issues within us first. We are always presented with an opportunity to clear issues within ourselves with any new challenge we face in life. Self-Reiki will also soothe the feelings of desperation around this job change and help create more peace.

Remember to meditate on the Reiki principles each day, either immediately before you self-treat, or while you are doing self-Reiki. This alone may be enough to help shift the way you feel about the situation and clear any blockages you have with regard to your work.

Also consider journaling about what your feelings are. Let Reiki flow into each journaling session, for the greatest and highest good, prior to writing. Explore what your underlying emotions and thoughts are about your current job. Accept what you are feeling without judgment, trying not to push your feelings away or get further entangled in thoughts that reinforce them. Then try to find one thing to have gratitude for with regard to your current job.

Next, imagine what you would prefer to feel like in your work environment. What would you like it to feel like emotionally, physically and energetically? What would the people be like? Imagine all the aspects that would help you feel supported in your best workplace scenario as you let Reiki flow through you to the situation. Write all of it down in your journal. After you have finished, say a prayer of thanks to the Universe for helping you. Let go of any specific ideas you have about how this help will come to be. Be open to trusting the Universe and Reiki to bring it to you in the best possible way. Keep opening yourself to this trust each day, asking Reiki for help with being open when you need it.

Question 79

How can Reiki help me to find and settle with a good job, or a promotion at my current job?

Deb's answer:

As Universal Life Force Energy, Reiki is a source of unlimited possibilities. You can set any intention you would like, but also be aware to set every intention for your highest good. What this means is an acceptance of any outcome. As human beings, we have a narrow view of what would be best for us. It is impossible to know the whole picture; there may be reasons why you are not yet ready for a particular job or promotion. For example, if you set an intention that you must have a specific job, you may feel disappointed when it is offered to someone else. Perhaps, there is a better opportunity for you in the next few months, or the other person needs the position for unknown (to you) reasons.

The primary life purpose, for all of us, is to learn life lessons. During the course of our lifetimes, everyone has many lessons to learn. These lessons are as varied and numerous as snowflakes in a large mountain range. Maybe we need to learn acceptance of others' viewpoints, cooperation, using our voices appropriately, respect and compassion for all people, self-esteem, courage, and perseverance – the list is truly endless. We may also need to learn the expression of gratitude – gratitude for having the job we have right now, and gratitude for the opportunity to find a job that may be more fitting to our education, experience and individual preferences.

Continue using Reiki as a regular basis. The energetic balance that Reiki brings into your life will lead to the right job for you.

Chapter 15 – Healing the Past

Question 80

How do I heal past harm I have caused?

I understand that Reiki can be used to go back and heal situations that have occurred in the past. How is this carried out? For example, if you caused pain to somebody some years ago and you wanted to heal that, how would you go about it?

Angie's answer:

It is a very healing thing just that you are seeking to send healing to this situation. The simple intention that you have in your heart to heal the damage that occurred as a result of your actions is a powerful start to the healing process, both for yourself and for the other involved.

When we harm another, we harm ourselves, so it is always beneficial to send healing when we cause harm, even if the healing is unlikely to reverse the consequences of our previous action. It is best to send healing purely for the sake of healing, for soothing the energy of that past moment, rather than to send healing with an eye toward making someone forgive you, trust you or like you again.

To send Reiki to the past in this way, you can do it very similarly to sending any distant Reiki treatment. It may be easiest to use a proxy, such as an object or a stuffed animal, to represent the person you are sending Reiki to. When I send Reiki to past situations, I particularly like using a rose quartz, but you can hold any object you like. It is simply something for your mind and hands to focus on. Draw the symbols over the object you have chosen and hold in your mind and heart the time you wish to send healing to and invite Reiki to flow.

At first, send healing to your own past woundedness; that pain that allowed you to harm another. Forgive yourself. You may wish to place one hand over your own heart as you work with Reiki during this portion of the exercise. It may help to see your present self, assisting your past self in healing, possibly even seeing your present self in that room in the past sending Reiki and guidance to your former self.

Next, send Reiki to the one you harmed. Invite that person's higher self or guides to assist in the healing, to heal any harm done on all levels. Ask Reiki to heal any pain or grief resulting from this situation through all of time and space. Ask that you both receive any growth or guidance that may be possible from the situation and leave the damage behind. If you are particularly good at visualization, you may wish to place Reiki symbols in the room where the damage occurred, as well, though this is not necessary.

I appreciate your question. Healing the past, especially taking responsibility for healing our own past, is a very special and noble step in healing the present and the future of us all. I commend you for attending to this.

Question 81

How to heal a past life trauma?

I have a client who wants some help healing a past life trauma. He has a large birthmark on his arms that his intuition tells him is from a severe burn that never healed properly in a past life of his. Can you suggest some specific Reiki symbols to use with regards to healing this karmic scar?

Patti's answer:

Healing past life trauma can be accomplished by sending Reiki back in time to a past situation. The distance symbol, Hon Sha Ze Sho Nen, is the symbol used to send Reiki through time and space. Used with intent, symbols focus healing to a specific area or issue, often with powerful results. Draw or visualize Hon Sha Ze Sho Nen while consciously setting the intent to cut all cords to past trauma and release all that no longer serves the highest good.

Have your client set their intent by repeating a mantra such as: *I give myself permission to let this go. I release all that no longer serves me.*

Chapter 16 – Death

Question 82

Can Reiki assist a client to pass over more easily?

Deb's answer:

Reiki has many benefits for people who are transitioning from this life to the next life. For the physical body, Reiki can reduce any pain associated with the disease process, or anxieties related to breathing difficulties or other changes in the body. It can also alleviate any fears the person may be experiencing and bring peace to their last moments on earth. Because the dying person is the only one experiencing this journey at that moment in time, being touched in such a loving and gentle way through Reiki is very comforting.

Also, consider giving Reiki to family members or other loved ones who are sharing in this difficult transition. Many times, the dying person has difficulty in "letting go" due to their concerns about leaving loved ones behind. As loved ones become more accepting of the impending death, it is easier for the person's spirit to release his physical body.

Many people believe that previously deceased loved ones, angels and other spirit beings greet the dying and help them to transition to the spiritual world. Because Reiki helps all of us to become more connected with this realm, it certainly helps the dying to experience this beautiful connection.

Question 83

Is there any special way to administer healing during final days of someone?

Ashwita's answer:

The best way to heal a person during their final days is through intuition. Any strong blocks in a person's energy field will prevent their energy from leaving the body smoothly. You can also try talking to her and see if you get any clues as to which chakras might need healing.

For example, if you sense that they are quite afraid then you know that it is a good idea to heal the root and solar plexus chakras and the knees. If they seem to have difficulty communicating what they are feeling, the throat chakra needs healing. If there seem to be unresolved issues with loved ones, then the heart chakra needs healing. I recommend healing all the chakras in the front as well as the back of the body. The back chakras in this case are especially important as this is where the suppressed emotions are stored, and are what the soul will carry with it.

Lastly, I would recommend starting the healing from the lower chakras and moving upwards, instead of the usual top-down sequence.

Question 84

Can Reiki be given to the departed souls?

Can Reiki be given to the departed souls so that they can attain some kind of solace?

Haripriya's answer:

Yes, Reiki can definitely be sent to departed souls. It is the soul's choice whether to receive this healing or not. However, from our end, we can most certainly send Reiki to departed souls for solace and healing.

Question 85

Why is that I have a fear of death?

I would like to know why is that I have a fear of death?
In our Reiki class our master asked us to answer a few questions in our workbooks and one of them was "Do you see death as a failure?" My answer was yes. I have a fear of the unknown and I am scared of seeing a spirit being.
Perhaps you can enlighten me.

Patti's answer:

Death is a weighty subject, but I will do my best.

It is natural to have a fear of the unknown, and death is the ultimate unknown in our human existence. No one is immortal. No one escapes death's transition. And unless we have some psychic ability to communicate with those who have passed, what happens when our life ends here in this plane is left up to our (sometimes overactive) imaginations.

In becoming attuned to Reiki, my outlook toward death has undergone a gradual revision, in part because I have become more attuned with nature. In the natural world, nothing is wasted. We watch varieties of trees and flowers transition with the seasons. They move from seed, to stalk, to blossom; they fade and seemingly die, only to come back to life in the spring. In our own human existence, we see babies born, grow to discover the wonders of the earth, then mature to where they become concerned with worldly matters. Inevitably, their sense of wonder pales as they begin to be concerned with survival and making a living. We learn, we grow, and in time, we die, leaving the next generation to carry on and bring fresh perspective to our ever evolving world.

How many truly wonderful people have you encountered in your lifetime that have since passed on? Do you really believe their lovely spirit is gone forever? Or is it more likely that their light lives on, freed from a physical body that may be aged or diseased?

We would not want to live forever. There are not enough resources on our beautiful earth to sustain eternal life and so the cycle, or recycle if you will, continues.

Death as a failure? I think it is more of a step into the next experience. Have you ever had a sense of déjà vu as you enter a room or garden where you know you have never been? Or felt that someone you were just meeting seemed somehow familiar? Explore the idea that your spirit may have lived before - perhaps even many times.

Try out the idea of death as the ending of one journey and the start of another. Take your time. Opening to new ideas is a process. These are beliefs that are unique to each individual and you must discover your own. Open your mind and heart, and ask Spirit to guide you. The answers will come when you are ready.

In regard to your fear of seeing a spirit being. Not to worry, spirits rarely appear to us unless we are open to them. Even then, we always have control over what beings travel with us. A spirit cannot stay where it is not wanted. If a spirit appears to you and you wish it to leave, simply state out loud, "Please leave. You are not wanted here". However, if you release your fear and allow a good spirit to stay, you may be pleasantly surprised by the experience.

Chapter 17 – Angels

Question 86

How can I connect with my guardian angel?

During my second Reiki session, my companion friend saw a person while giving Reiki to me. My teacher told me that it is my guardian angel but refrained to give more details about it. I really want to know how can I connect with my guardian angel?

Deb's answer:

You are already connected to your guardian angel! This angel has been with you this entire lifetime, from the moment of your birth. What I think you might be asking is how you can see your guardian angel, or how you know your guardian angel is with you. The most important aspect is your awareness of his presence. (Although I am using the male gender pronouns, angels have no gender.) People become aware of guardian angels in different ways. Some people receive an inspirational thought and know it is from an angel. Some people may actually hear words spoken to them. Others can see angels through their third eye chakra. It is possible to carry on conversations with guardian angels and "listen" for a response.

Frequent Reiki practice, both as a giver and a receiver, heightens our awareness of all spiritual beings. Our intuitive abilities grow, and our understanding of the spirit world expands. Become familiar with all angelic beings, from the individual guardian angel to the hierarchies of all angels. You can do this through reading books, listening to webinars, looking at art work, talking to others, etc. The more knowledgeable and aware you become, the more you will realize angels are always with you.

Chapter 18 – Spirituality

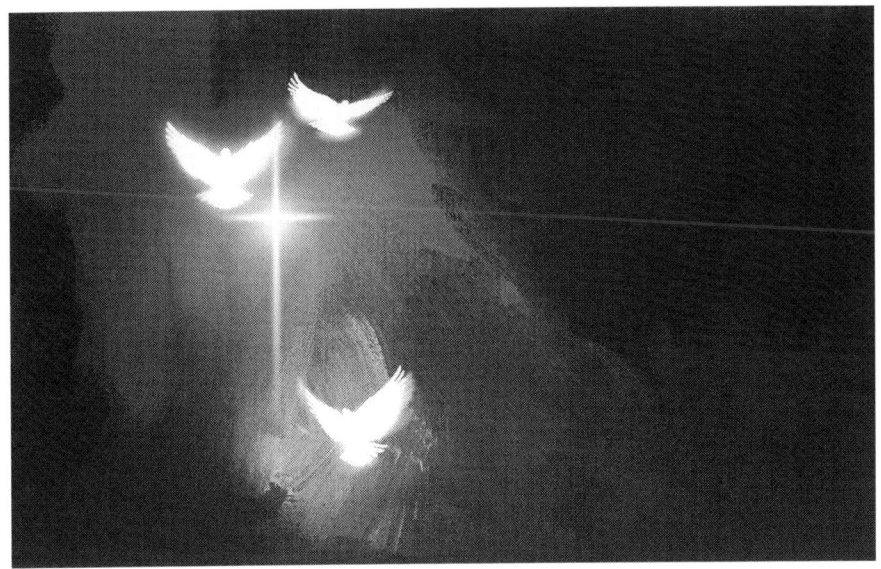

Question 87

What is the difference between Reiki and Spiritual Healing?

Patti's answer:

Reiki is a Japanese system of stress reduction and relaxation that promotes healing by tapping into universal life force energy. Some levels use symbols to connect to that energy. In order to be a Reiki healer you must be attuned by a teacher who is a Reiki Master. Reiki utilizes connection to spirit guides and universal energy, but does not include prayer to any deities.

"Spiritual healing" is a broad term that means different things to different people. It can be inclusive of religious practices and counseling. It usually involves the use of prayer to heal not only at the physical level, but to also focus on the spiritual growth of the individual.

While there can be a spiritual aspect to Reiki, it does not include specific religious practice.

Question 88

What is the difference between Reiki and the Divine / God?

Haripriya's answer:

In the simplest of terms, the Divine is Absolute Oneness. The building block of existence is just one energy. This means that everything in the Universe is connected to everything else. However, this energy manifests at different frequencies and at each frequency, it serves a different purpose. This can be compared to natural energies like wind, water, sunshine etc. Each of these energies has manifested differently and serves a different purpose but they are all related at a deeper level. Reiki is one such higher manifestation of the Divine. Other healing energies like Angelic energies, Violet Flame etc. hold different frequencies. However, all of them are interconnected and a manifestation of the one divine energy.

Question 89

Does Reiki have any connection with Jesus?

Patti's answer:

Reiki is not connected with Jesus, nor is it affiliated with any religion. However, there are similarities between the type of hands on healing performed by Jesus and the Reiki hands on healing method we use today. One major difference being that Jesus performed some pretty spectacular miracles with his hands on healing. As Reiki healers we provide universal life force energy for stress reduction and relaxation, which allows the body to clear imbalances and promotes healing. While the healing Reiki provides can be remarkable and miraculous, the stunning "arise and walk again" healing scenario does not apply.

Chapter 19 – Miscellaneous

Question 90

My Reiki training only took 4 hours. Is my Reiki as good as others' who have done 2 days?

Patti's answer:

Reiki training varies from one Reiki Master to another as far as timing, price and content. When choosing a Reiki trainer, always take the time to compare what is available and verify that it includes the content you seek. Reiki training should include a comprehensive overview of the material, a handout of written material to refer to later, the Reiki attunement, and ample time to practice and ask questions.

One thing that affects the length of a Reiki class is the size of the class. A large class will take longer, as there may be more questions and extra practice time. Larger groups also have to build in time for each student to be attuned. A small class with one on one attention can accomplish more in a shorter time frame.

A Reiki attunement for one person does not take up a lot of time. If the material is reviewed in detail and time has been allowed for questions, 4 hours is a reasonable amount of time.

Question 91

What is Breath Reiki?

I hear talk about Breath Reiki, I would like to know more about it, my guides sometimes have me breathe over an area. Is that the same thing?

Angie's answer:

This technique was called Koki-ho in Japan, but it is seldom called that or taught in the West. Many are guided to use the breath to send Reiki or to clear blocked energy or cords and it is very effective to assist in these.

The method consists of drawing Reiki energy into the breath, as a way of concentrating and focusing it, and then blowing the energy onto the area that is in need. Some Reiki Masters use this method as part of the attunement process. It sounds like what you have been guided to do is the same process, which you have been doing intuitively.

Question 92

What does it mean to infuse something with Reiki?

What does it mean to infuse something with Reiki, and are there ways to infuse recordings of music or videos with Reiki? Does it mean simply to focus Cho Ku Rei on it or Hon Sha Ze Sho Nen, or a sandwich of symbols?

Ashwita's answer:

Reiki works with intent, so to infuse anything with Reiki simply means that we intend that the use of that object facilitates Reiki healing. It is not so much the symbols, but the intent that is critical in infusing anything with Reiki.

Not just books, music or videos, we can also infuse food with Reiki, clothes, especially uncomfortable ones, pillows and eye masks for better sleep, massage oils, yoga mats, candles, essences, and the list goes on.

If it is an object you want to infuse with Reiki, hold it in your hands or place your hands over it if it is big. Let Reiki flow into it and request Reiki to flow to anyone who uses this object (or any other intention you might want Reiki's help with). If it is a file on your computer that you want to infuse with Reiki, do the same while placing your hands on the computer, or through distant healing.

If you have learned level 2, you could mentally all draw the symbols while you do this. Use Hon Sha Ze Sho Nen followed by Sei He Ki and Cho Ku Rei.

Question 93

Why is it advised to receive Reiki from others, like a Reiki circle, even though self-treatments are performed regularly?

Deb's answer:

When a person is doing self-treatments of Reiki, the Reiki energies flow and wonderful results can occur. When a Reiki practitioner is simply a receiver of Reiki, versus being both a giver and a receiver, there does seem to be a more powerful flow of Reiki energies. Perhaps, the reason is as basic as the person is not performing two roles at the same time.

One explanation may be that as a receiver one can achieve a higher level of relaxation and not have to think at all about when or where to place her hands during the treatment. It is easier to fall into a meditative state. The giver can maintain an objective focus and may more easily receive intuitive impressions about the receiver's energy levels, or areas of concern. The receiver can passively accept the healing energies while the giver is more actively engaged in treatment aspects.

When a Reiki practitioner receives Reiki, the energies are very strong. The attunements may enhance the receiving experience. It is a gift to give and receive Reiki with another practitioner. Many practitioners find a Reiki buddy and exchange sessions on a regular basis. What a beautiful blessing to both people!

Question 94

How long will the Reiki energy stay in an object?

If you use Reiki in something like a blanket how long will the Reiki energy stay in the material without any Reiki maintenance?

Haripriya's answer:

It all depends on the intention you set. If you do not set an intention, Reiki will follow a natural course and the flow will stop once the intended purpose is served. This may take a few minutes or hours.

However, it is possible to program the energy to stay for a specific time period without needing to consciously give Reiki throughout. One way to achieve this is to write out your request to Reiki on a piece of paper. Remember to specify the time period for which you wish Reiki to flow. Draw the distance symbol on the paper and pin it to the blanket (or any other object). This will ensure that the energy continues to flow long after you stop channeling it.

Question 95

Why are my dreams so vivid since I have resumed self-treatment?

Why are my dreams so vivid and of a strange nature now that I have resumed self treatment? When I awake I don't worry about those dreams I only wonder why and hope your answer will bring me to a better understanding of what is happening.

Angie's answer:

It is very likely that the vivid dreams are simply a by-product of energy clearing and processing now that you have resumed self-treatment. They will probably balance out as you continue to do regular self-treatment.

Question 96

Can Reiki be used to harm people?

I would like to know if Reiki can be used to harm people, or in a bad way.
I learned that Reiki energy can only be used for good uses, just like I read in your website, but some days ago, I heard someone (Reiki practitioner) tell me about people who used Reiki in another way, that it could be used to harm people or to make things go wrong to that person.

Angie's answer:

I have not heard of Reiki being used in this manner. Reiki is a healing aspect of Universal Life Force energy. However, all energy is energy, which is neither "good" nor "bad." The intention with which you attempt to use it can be malicious or benevolent. This is true of everything we do, in all aspects of life.

When we choose to do something for the purpose of the greatest good, we are bringing greater energy to us and to the situation we are working with. The energy we send out is what we generate to return to us in everything we do. The same is true if we have malevolent intent and choose to harm or manipulate someone. We are sending out negative energy, which narrows energy pathways and generates the same energy to return to us and to the situation we are working with. It is not a wise thing to do.

Reiki practitioners are taught that their own self-healing is the primary thing they must focus on, in order to be proper healers for others. We cannot effectively do self-healing if we are bringing negative energy back to ourselves. So, while I don't personally know of Reiki being used this way, my advice is not to attempt it. Reiki is a healing energy and in all likelihood it would not work when used maliciously, in any event. Energy works best when we let go of ego and allow the greatest good to come through us.

Question 97

Is there such a thing as 'overloading' yourself with Reiki energy?

Is there such a thing as 'overloading' yourself with Reiki energy? Let's say I am using Reiki on my throat area and Reiki is not required on that area, will I be 'overloading' it with energy or will it just go to different parts of the body?

Haripriya's answer:

There is no such thing as 'overloading' yourself with Reiki.

Reiki is life force energy and carries the innate intelligence of the Universe at its core. Being an intelligent energy, Reiki knows where to flow and also how much to flow. Once an area receives the amount of Reiki it needs, the flow of Reiki to that area automatically stops. Reiki then flows where it is needed next.

Being regular with Reiki practice increases one's sensitivity to the energy. This helps you intuitively gauge when an area has received sufficient Reiki and you are spontaneously guided to move your palms to the next position.

Question 98

How do I heal effects I feel during Full Moon?

I am very sensitive to a certain moon effects, especially full moon time. I feel horrible, feel angry, very low and just wish I never existed. I am a Reiki channel. How do I heal this and does using symbols in specific sequence make a difference?

Ashwita's answer:

I have observed that people who have picked up negative energies from others tend to fluctuate very widely during new and full moons. You might want to make a few sacred fires every evening – maybe for 21 days even, or at least smudge your living space with sage everyday for a while till you feel better.

If you are in the habit of using plenty of crystals, try putting them all in a bag and setting them in a corner before you do the cleansing, and if the crystals are contributing to your instability, that would make quite an instant difference. If this is not the case, you can cleanse the crystals thoroughly and place them back.

A firm grounding ensures you don't fluctuate. So spend plenty of time in nature, do some gardening and give plenty of healing to the lower three chakras, both in the front as well as back.

Question 99

Is this possible to learn or practice Reiki during pregnancy?

Ashwita's answer:

The role of Reiki begins even before pregnancy. Many childless couples who learn Reiki together, conceive quite easily after a few weeks (or even days, in some instances). Reiki is also wonderful when learned or practiced during pregnancy, as it minimizes the nausea and discomfort.

During pregnancy, the emotional and mental state of the mother affects the growth of the child. Regular Reiki practice brings stability in not just this regard but also physical health, and obviously benefits the child. In case the mother-to-be is exposed to emotionally difficult situations during pregnancy, Reiki practice helps to clear out the negative energies picked up and prevents the baby from being influenced by them.

I have also observed that children carrying difficult energies either from a past life or due to other reasons can be healed during pregnancy so that they have much clearer energies by the time they are born. On multiple occasions I have found a baby in the womb to have very low, sick energies (in some cases because the parents weren't in love and in others because the mother was struggling to cope with a difficult life at the time). Through regular Reiki practice however, the baby's energies showed a remarkable improvement by the time of delivery, and the energies cleared completely over the year after birth. However, in my observation the pregnancy is harder in such cases, as the mother takes up the trauma of the baby to help it release – so if a mother is unwilling to take up any trauma for the child she must clearly intend so.

The delivery is also much easier for women practicing and receiving Reiki. Some women I know had just 15 minutes of labor!

Question 100

What's with the negative messages on Reiki on the Internet?

Sometimes the net shows very negative messages on Reiki, which can discourage people to do Reiki.

Patti's answer:

You do not have to look far on the Internet to find negativity on any subject, and Reiki is no exception. Your best guide is always the manual and information given to you by your Reiki Master. Feel free to explore information on Reiki and different modalities on the Internet, however if you always return to your traditional Reiki training materials and resources, you will not be confused or misled by hype or misinformation.

Chapter 20 – Life Purpose

Question 101

Is there a way to use Reiki to help determine your Life Purpose?

Is there a way to use Reiki to help determine your Life Purpose / Path? I've heard you just follow your passion, but I really don't have any one passion. I feel like an untethered balloon at times. Any suggestions?

Angie's answer:

Sometimes we have to make room for things to flow a bit more than our logical minds might like, so it can be OK to feel like an untethered balloon at times! Over time, you will probably find that you are led to put your energy into a few things at a time for a while and then your focus may shift. This can be channeled into family, work, volunteer activities, activism, art or other things. Life purpose is certainly not limited to what makes money! Though money is necessary, we are here for far more than that.

To use Reiki to help you determine your life purpose, you can set the intention to be on your life path, following your purpose and allow Reiki to flow to this. I recommend that you do this in two ways. First, write the intention down on a piece of paper. On this paper, also write the things in life that make you happy and bring you joy when you are doing them. These are the things that you simply lose yourself in and possibly lose track of time while you are involved in them. Include things that you do for fun, for yourself, for others and for your community. It's totally fine to have more than one thing that brings you great joy! Also write down at least 3 things that describe how you would like your life to feel. These should ideally be emotionally charged words or phrases. You are trying to tap into the emotional energy of the future life you wish to create, so really feel what you want experience that as. Send Reiki to this list and intention and look at it once a week to see how things are shifting.

Second, each morning when you wake up, let Reiki begin to flow forward into your day. Set the intention that you will be open to your purpose and your path and that you will be open to and aware of any nudges from your intuition. Ask Reiki to guide you and make your way open and clear. Intend to be wise and discerning, yet open and allowing. The longer you do this practice, the easier it will be to trust that you are on your life path. You will begin to see signs and you will start to understand your intuition more and more.

About the Authors

Angie Webster *works with energy healing, offering Reiki sessions, as well as teaching Reiki classes and animal Reiki. As a freelance writer, she regularly writes about Reiki and spirituality. She constantly seeks to expand her understanding of the way energy works in the body and in our world and to share that with others through her writing and her teaching. Angie's hope in her work and her life is to help others find their way to greater balance and their own innate healing capabilities. Angie is the author of* **Infinite Reiki, Infinite Healing: How Energy Medicine Healed my Life and What It Can do for Yours.** *Reiki and a healthy lifestyle contributed to her healing after a 20 year struggle with neurological and chronic pain issues. She comes out the other side with a new perspective on life. Angie has been a regular contributor at Reiki Rays (www.reikirays.com) since 2013 and has also contributed to Elephant Journal, Rebelle Society and Be You Media (www.beyoumediagroup.com).*

You can contact Angie at: http://www.serenityenergyhealing.com/
https://www.facebook.com/HolisticSpirituality/?fref=ts
https://naturalholisticlife.wordpress.com/

Patti Deschaine *is a traditionally trained Usui Reiki Master, Lightarian Reiki Master, and owner of Maja Energy Works and Reiki Healing. She resides and practices in Wilmington, NC. She enjoys all types of Reiki and particularly loves using Reiki on animals.*

Patti can be found at http://majaenergyworksandreikihealing.com/ *and on Facebook at:* https://www.facebook.com/MajaEnergyWorks.

Haripriya Suraj is a Reiki Master, Angel Healer, and Spiritual Teacher. She was drawn to Reiki right from her childhood and Reiki went on to become part of her life's purpose. Reiki is her constant companion from which she derives peace and contentment. After reaping the fruits of Reiki practice in her life, she was inspired to spread the joy of Reiki. She is the founder of Aananda Holistic Center where she conducts as well as teaches Reiki and Angel Healing. Haripriya resides in Bangalore, India.

Reach Haripriya at aanandaholistic@gmail.com and at Aananda Holistic Center on Facebook.

Deborah Lloyd *is a Usui and Karuna® Reiki Master and certified holistic therapy practitioner. She also is a licensed clinical social worker, working with a hospice agency in Asheville, NC. She grew up on a farm in rural Indiana and was stricken with polio at the age of three. To relieve fatigue from post-polio syndrome, she learned Reiki. This complementary technique led her to explore other alternative modalities. Her personal journey, along with life lessons learned along the way, is detailed in her book,* **Believe and it is True: A Story of Healing and Life Lessons**.

Reach Deborah at http://www.deblloydhealing.com/, *deb@deblloydhealing.com, at*
Deb Lloyd Healing on Facebook -
https://www.facebook.com/deblloydhealing, *and on* Twitter *at* https://twitter.com/deblloydhealing

Having learned Meditation as a child, **Ashwita Goel** incorporated Reiki into her life during her early teens. After a decade of witnessing the magic Reiki, she felt compelled to take up Reiki professionally, and ended her corporate career in 2007, taking up Reiki full-time. She eventually incorporated EFT, hypnotherapy and past life therapy into her work. Apart from her healing work, she teaches Reiki and meditation, and her book '**Healing Through Reiki**' is available on Amazon.

You can connect with Ashwita through Facebook https://www.facebook.com/Reiki.Bangalore, her website http://www.reiki-bangalore.com/ or visit her blog http://www.ashwita.com/zen/.

Printed in Great Britain
by Amazon